SUCCEEDING IN ENEMY TERRITORY

by David A. Seamands

First released under the title *Living with Your Dreams*

Mansfield, PA

To

our children

Sharon

Steve

Debbie

MK's

who

by the grace of God

became OK's

and

helped fulfill our family dreams

PREFACE

The overarching theme of this book is how God works in all things, even the seemingly little ones, to fulfill the dreams He implants in us, causing us to succeed even though we now live in enemy territory. What is that success? Seeing His purposes accomplished through our lives. In view of this, I want to thank those whom God has used so significantly in widening my ministry.

I have always had a dream about writing—don't most preachers and missionaries?—but could not seem to get started. In the late 1970s this dream was reinforced by a strong impression that the inner voice of the Holy Spirit was saying, "Start writing." But I was unable to overcome the fears from another voice, my inner child of the past, which countered with, "Don't be silly; no one would read it and then you'd look like a fool." Sad to say, this veto of immobilizing fear kept me from being obedient to the heavenly vision. God knew I needed something from the outside to push me off dead center and get me going.

And so, in His gracious providence, God led a young woman named Cathy Streeter to enroll at Asbury College. This was very unusual because she lived in the shadow of several other outstanding Christian colleges where she could have gone. After a few weeks of attending my church, she wrote her mother about her new pastor whom she thought might be a possible author. It just happened that her mother was Carole Streeter, an acquisitions editor at Victor Books. She not only urged me to write, but kept on encouraging me, even when I delayed for almost two years. Finally, she made an unusual offer—to transcribe and edit directly off my sermon cassettes. That did it.

The result of this preacher-to-daughter-to-mother-to-publisher contact was the publication of *Healing for Damaged Emotions* in 1981, and several subsequent books on emotional and spiritual healing. My heartfelt thanks go to Cathy and Carole for becoming so involved in my

God-given dreams. However, the story isn't over. A new chapter continues to illustrate the providence of God so beautifully expressed in the words of William Cowper's familiar hymn, "God works in a mysterious way His wonders to perform."

Recently, two fans of my writings who work for Kingdom Publishing discovered that a particular book of mine was out of print. An editor with Kingdom called Asbury Theological Seminary and finally tracked me down to our home in Florida, where we had been living since retirement. From the first phone call, there was agreement "in the Spirit" that the message of the book was more needed than ever. We also felt its title should better express the active nature of the high and holy dreams required of us as we enter the 21ˢᵗ century. And so, *Succeeding in Enemy Territory* became a reality.

David A. Seamands
Nokomis, Florida
1999

1

HERE COMES THE DREAMER

There's one in almost every family, isn't there? There's one kid who's different: one who stands out from the others, and not necessarily because of beauty or handsomeness. No, not so much in *looks*, but in *outlook*—different in the way the youngster looks *to* others and *at* others. Such children are seen differently and so see things differently. Or is it the other way around? Perhaps because they perceive life differently, they are perceived differently. Probably it works both ways, each helping to feed and, in turn, be fed by the other.

Often these kids come from warm and wonderful family backgrounds; but sometimes it is quite the opposite and everyone wonders how they got to be the way they are. No doubt there are many elements, known and unknown, which work together to make them different.

If we look closely, I believe we will discover that one of the key factors is this: Somewhere along the line these people were captured and captivated by a dream. There is an idea that motivates them, an ideal that moves them in the direction of a certain goal. In one sense, this dream—call it a vision or an aspiration if you like—is like the driving force of a motor, pushing them from the inside. In another sense, it is like the drawing force of a magnet, pulling them from the outside and causing them to succeed, even when they're in enemy territory. We can see it in almost any area of life, but we see it most clearly in the realm of sports—maybe because in that arena it is so easily observed and even measured.

In his book *The Heart of a Champion*, Olympic medallist Bob Richards illustrates just how important such a dream really is, as he tells about the famous runner, Charley Paddock. One day while speaking in the assembly at a Cleveland high school, Charley said, "Who knows, we may even have an Olympic champ right here in this hall!" Afterward, a skinny, spindly-legged youngster who had been hanging around the edge of the crowd came up and said to him very shyly, "I'd give anything if I could become a championship runner someday." Charley Paddock answered him warmly, "You can, son, you can, if you'll make it your goal and give it your all." In 1936 that young man, whose name was Jessie Owens, won gold medals and broke records in the Munich Olympics. Adolph Hitler watched his stunning performance and was infuriated, for the fulfillment of that young African-American's dream did as much as anything to smash Hitler's horrible dream of a superior Aryan race.

When Jessie Owens came home, he was given a hero's welcome. That day another spindly-legged black youngster squeezed his way through the crowds and said, "I'd sure like to grow up and become a runner in the Olympics someday." Jessie remembered and grabbed the kid's hand. He said, "Dream big, son; dream big. And give it all you've got." In 1948, Harrison Dillard also won gold medals at the Olympics.[1]

Another sports illustration is the story of a high school student who was practicing the high jump in preparation for the state contest. Each time he jumped, his coach would raise the bar up a little higher. Finally, he put it up to the record height for that event. The teenager protested, "Aw come on, Coach, how do you think I can ever jump *that* high?" The coach replied, "Just throw your heart over the bar first and the rest of you will follow."

Our most satisfying examples of overcoming obstacles in order to reach the goal are found in Scripture. Jesus hinted that there is something that even precedes the heart. "For where your treasure is, there your heart will be also" (Matthew 6:21). If *heart* reflects desires, then *treasure* represents the value we put on the object of those desires. It is the prize, the goal, the treasure for which we are willing to pay any price. It is at this deepest level where our dreams operate—those treasured dreams which fill our hearts and fuel our desires.

Dreams are contagious. One person's dreams can infect a crowd of people and inspire them to move toward the same goal—even when the odds are such that pursuit of the goal would normally seem futile. I personally experienced the infectious power of a dream some years ago. It was early in 1963, and my family and I had recently returned home from our sixteen years of missionary work in India. I was in my first year of the pastorate and, along with a small handful of pastors and laypersons, had been working very hard to get the public schools of our county racially integrated. There had been a lot of opposition, and I was getting discouraged. Consequently, one cold winter day I marched with several thousands who had come from all over the state to take part in a rally on the steps of the Kentucky state capitol.

I had heard a lot about the speaker of the day and was hoping he might further our cause. He began by surveying the civil-rights movement all over the country and summarizing some of its goals. Then, slowly but inexorably, like a symphony increasing in intensity, his words and emotions gained momentum. I sensed a change as the crowd began to stir and to express their own feelings audibly. I had seen something like this in India during the struggle for independence, and I knew what could happen to a large mass of people. So I decided I would remain strictly an observer. I would not allow myself to become a participant. Whatever the others did, I would remain detached and objective.

But then Dr. Martin Luther King, Jr. reached his crescendo. "I HAVE A DREAM!" he shouted exultantly, and tearing his own heart wide open so we could all peer inside, he showed us a picture of that dream. Again and again he repeated the resounding refrain "I HAVE A DREAM! ... I HAVE A DREAM!"

Each time he said this, he would include a fiery quotation from an Old Testament prophet and add one more picture of the dream. Finally, like a movie camera zooming in closer and closer until its object fills the whole wide screen, he showed us the full picture of his dreamscape. It was so electrifying that I found myself clapping and shouting, "Amen ... Yes ... That's right ... Amen!" It was an unforgettable experience. That day I learned the awesome power of an awe-inspiring dream, and I returned home uplifted and encouraged.

In late 1989, the world again witnessed the irresistible force of the great dream of freedom. We were thrilled as we saw the cold war melting, barbed-wire fences being pulled up and concrete walls being torn down. We watched incredulously as many persons literally went from prison to palace. Again and again we heard people tearfully but joyously say, "We've dreamed about this moment for years."

When we try to explain such happenings with, "Nothing can stop the power of an idea whose time has come," we are simply paying tribute to the driving force of a dream. Without a dream or a vision people really do perish; but with one they withstand persecution, persist through opposition, and pursue the prize with perseverance.

Young Man with a Dream

Nowhere is the importance of the dream more striking than in the Biblical account of Joseph, who comes to life in Genesis, chapter 30. In Genesis 37, when Joseph has reached the age of 17, we are reminded how important dreams were in his life.

- "Joseph had a dream" (verse 5)
- "And they hated him all the more because of his dream" (verse 8)
- "Then he had another dream" (verse 9)
- "His father rebuked him and said, "What is this dream you had?" (verse 10)
- "Here comes the dreamer! ... Come now, let us kill him, then we'll see what comes of his dreams" (verse 19, 20)

Joseph had dreams when he was asleep; but because they were so strong and vivid, they became the compelling vision of his life when he was awake. Basically, these were dreams of God's blessing upon Joseph's life, bringing a vision that he would be put into a place of leadership and authority. Although the dream-vision seemed utterly unrealistic, Joseph never forgot it, never doubted it, and never abandoned it. Even when it seemed completely shattered by unscrupulous enemies and ungrateful companions, by unbearable humiliation and unjust suffering, it set before him a high and holy goal. The dream also gave him the power to keep moving toward that goal, and filled him with the quiet confidence that God was always with him and was somehow working to bring about the dream's fulfillment.

As they say, "The rest is history." In this book, we will follow the remarkable unfolding of Joseph's story for our model of succeeding in enemy territory. From a purely human standpoint, it is as interesting and exciting as any story written. Many years ago Thomas Mann based his several-volume, classic novel on the life of Joseph. But because this is also God's story, we shall discover through it some of the most important lessons that God's Word has to teach us. Paul tells us, "All Scripture is God-breathed and is useful for teaching, rebuking, correcting and training in righteousness" (2 Timothy 3:16). But as Peter reminds us, using Paul's very own writings as an example, the Scriptures also "contain some things that are hard to understand" (2 Peter 3:16). What makes the story of Joseph so appealing is that it delivers the inspired Scripture to us in such fascinating wrappings. This is one reason why Joseph proves equally exciting to preschool children and senior citizens.

Before we go any further, I want to emphasize that this book is not a study of sleep dreams or how to interpret them. I am not belittling such dreams, for they were one of the major ways by which God communicated with people in Bible times. Some personal experiences I have had, both in my own spiritual pilgrimage and in my counseling-healing ministry, convince me that God still does, at times, speak to us through such means. Interestingly enough, the Scriptures do not make a clear-cut distinction between dreams, visions, appearances of angels or messengers, and even unique incidents of being "in the Spirit."

In this book, however, when I speak about dreams and visions, I am referring to the pictures on the screens of our minds, which hold before us certain goals and give us a strong desire to reach them. One does not have to be a Christian, or even particularly religious, to have a dream and to experience its power to motivate and energize life. That's why I have used illustrations from many kinds of people.

My main concern, however, is to help Christians, first, understand how to recognize the dreams God has given, and second, discover how to successfully realize those dreams even

> *Our main interest is not how God gave the dream to us, but what He wants to accomplish through it.*

though often moving through enemy territory. We may have to ask God to restore our dreams, which have been shattered by the stresses of life. Furthermore, as Christians, we can look at a dream from many standpoints and call it by many different names: a high and holy ideal, an aspiration toward some desired goal, a compelling idea or plan we would like to carry out. Sometimes the dream is a cause about which we feel strongly, a call to a particular kind or place of service, or a vision of what we would like to accomplish in that service. Our main interest is not how God gave the dream to us, but what He wants to accomplish through it. For example, Joseph got his *dream* through *dreams*, and Paul got his *vision* through a *vision*. Regarding Cornelius and the Gentiles, Peter received his *instructions* through something like a *daydream* ("trance" in the NIV translation of Acts 10:10), while Cornelius received his *instructions* through *"an angel of God"* (Acts 10:3).

Today we have the complete written Word of Scripture as well as Christ, the Living Word. We also have the inner voice of the Holy Spirit now present and active in new ways; the truths of our ever-expanding knowledge of God's created world; and the corporate wisdom and guidance of the church, the body of Christ in this world. God can and does implant His dream for us through any and all of these ways. What's important is not how we get a dream, but whether we have one, and whether we will allow God to work in our lives so that He can accomplish what He had in mind when He gave it to us.

This is why, in spite of the many differences of time and historical setting, the story of Joseph still provides our best illustration and greatest inspiration. For it shows so clearly Joseph's unswerving commitment to be faithful to the dream, and God's unwavering commitment to fulfill it.

Is Joseph Too Good?

Before we go any further, let me share with you my greatest concern in basing a book on Joseph. If you are familiar with his story, perhaps you have already thought of it too. Can we really learn much from Joseph's life? Isn't he just a little *too* good? Maybe not perfect, but pretty close to it? With good reason he has been called the most Christlike figure in the Old Testament. He seems to do everything just right, never yielding to temptation, never falling or faltering, never doubting or breaking under the strain. So what can he really say to us—who do most, if not all, of the above? Ultimately, Joseph's dreams were fulfilled, while ours are broken and shattered.

What we should ask is not, "Is the story of Joseph too good to be true?" but "Is his life helpful or useful?" Helpful, that is, to so many of us who aren't very good? Useful to those of us who, unlike Joseph, have messed up God's dreams for our lives? Can God speak through this near-perfect Joseph to us not-so-perfect Joe's and Jane's? These are the kinds of questions I have been compelled to ask, because so much of my own personal Christian life and my ministry has been spent experiencing God's healing grace myself and then helping to bring His grace to bruised people with damaged emotions. So many people today need help in repairing their broken dreams and in rebuilding their shattered lives.

However, the more I prayed and listened, and the more deeply I dug into the details of the story, the more clearly the "eyes of my heart" (Ephesians 1:18) saw the true shape of the Spirit's dream for this book. I have always believed that one of the chief areas where the Holy Spirit works in our lives is in our subconscious minds—that deep inner layer of the mind through which God often wants to communicate with us.

For instance, while preparing to write this book, I awakened one morning to find my mind bubbling up with a lot of new thoughts. I quickly jotted them down in very rough form. After further reflection, I structured this book around them and hope they will answer some of the questions that we have been asking:

- Our dreams, aspirations, and visions are often God-given and are one of His ways of communicating with us. Through them, He wants to develop and use our uniqueness and gifts to accomplish His purposes.
- Those dreams sometimes become mixed with our own pride, selfishness, immaturity, and sin; they need to be purified, tested, matured, refined, and sometimes even refashioned.
- In this fallen, imperfect world, these dreams are often interrupted, broken, shattered, and unfulfilled. This can happen through the sins and choices of others, through events and circumstances over which we have no control, through our own sins and wrong choices, or by a combination of these factors.
- When our dreams are injured, God does not want us to abandon those dreams, but will lovingly work with us…

    to refine our unrealistic dreams

    to restore our broken dreams

    to realize our delayed dreams

    to redesign our shattered dreams…

so that both His purposes and our dreams can be fulfilled. I believe that the story of Joseph illuminates and illustrates these basic principles as clearly as any in Scripture because of its down-to-earth situations. As the Quakers like to say, "It speaks to our condition."

> *Both His purposes and our dreams can be fulfilled.*

An Ancient Family with a Modern Look

Too often we romanticize the Joseph story and look at it with rose-colored glasses. But when we do this, we miss some pertinent details through which God wants to speak to us.

For our present look at Joseph's family, we can't begin the story where most people do—at Genesis 37:2, where Joseph enters center stage as a young man of seventeen and begins his series of remarkable adventures. We will need to go back several chapters in Genesis to start our study. Unlike most of the other historical Old Testament books, the early chapters of Genesis do not follow a strict chronology. They go back and forth in time and skip from one character to another so that the time sequence does not follow the chapter sequence.

In order to use this book most powerfully in your own life, it will be helpful for you to spend a few minutes reviewing the Bible's account of Joseph's life. To understand the true background of the story, we should start reading in Genesis 29. Then we can take an honest look at the complicated "Jacob family" out of which Joseph came.

It doesn't take long to see that it was far less than an ideal situation. Actually, it was a family comprised of many inter-related families. There was one father, Jacob, with two wives, Leah and Rachel, who were sisters, together with their respective children. Two other women, Zilpah and Bilhah, who were the wives' maidservants, also had children by Jacob. These might be an ancient equivalent of what we think of today as surrogate mothers.

Thus, there is one father but multiple mothers, siblings, and half-siblings. Add to this a very large number of grandparents and half-grandparents, and you have quite an extended (though not very blended) family. As we read the graphic details from Genesis 29—35, we are struck by the selfishness, conflict, favoritism, jealousy, hatred, revenge, lust, rape, incest, deceit, and even mass murder. It's not exactly the Brady Bunch!

Back in the 1980's, a Sheik came to the United States for surgery, bringing with him his wives, children, and servants. He rented the entire floor of a hotel to house them. One newspaper called the entourage his family, but a *TIME* magazine reporter quipped that it was more like a menagerie. If we were to try to make a genogram or family chart of Joseph, it too might look like a menagerie.

I am deliberately stressing this aspect, for although the story is set in 2000 B.C., it is amazingly relevant for 2000 A.D. Of course, the sociological customs and patterns of that day were very different from ours, but the resulting family complications have many similarities.

In the USA today about fifty percent of those marrying for the first time will divorce. About sixty percent of those entering a second marriage also will divorce. In time, about seventy-five percent of these divorced persons will get remarried. Because of this continuing disintegration of today's families, approximately one-half of the children of our country spend part of their lives living with a step-parent and step-siblings.

I have had to deal, in my counseling ministry, with some of the tragic complexities which arise from what modern sociologists call the "serial polygamy" of divorce and remarriage. As couples share their stories with me, I have no problem understanding about "his," "her," and "our" children. But then I occasionally discover a child who doesn't seem to fit any of those categories, who turns out to be a "divorce orphan," a child who isn't the biological offspring of either of the currently-married spouses. This is a step-child who has been left behind at some point with one of the present partners when a prior husband or wife walked out and simply abandoned the child!

What is so amazing is that our God, the God of Abraham, Isaac, and Jacob, who chose such messed-up people to be His friends, seems to specialize in taking such mistakes and messes and making miracles out of them. God doesn't always do this the way we would want Him to—by instantly intervening in situations, changing the outer circumstances of people's lives so that they in turn can change. Most of the time He implants in their lives a transformed outlook—a dream, a vision, a powerful conviction—which first changes them so that they are then enabled to live *above* the circumstances and to become the means of changing situations. Some of you especially need this particular part of the Joseph story. I pray it will inspire and energize you to live out your dreams, *regardless of the family situation from which you have come.*

As we work through the story of Joseph, we will hear the same theme over and over again: God's incredible ability to bring good out of evil. The message stands out so clearly because, like the famous coat of many colors, the contrasts of Joseph's story are perhaps more vivid than those found in any other Scripture:

- the finest dreams and the fiercest obstacles
- the highest ideals and the deepest injustices
- the holiest determinations and the deadliest defeats
- the weirdest plots and the strangest twists

But, as we are reminded four times in Genesis 39, "The Lord was with Joseph," so that the biggest tragedies become the brightest triumphs! Now that's a message we all need to hear.

2

DREAMS NEED TEMPERING

In 1910, a tall, gangly eighteen-year-old named Arnett graduated from high school in Tucson, Arizona. His father was a train conductor and his older brothers were engineers on the railroad. The little religion they had in the home had disappeared when his mother died several years before. For as long as he could remember, Arnett had dreamed of being a civil engineer. But times were hard and his family could not afford the cost of such an expensive college education.

One day, Arnett heard that the Engineering College at the University of Cincinnati had a co-op course in civil engineering. This meant that he could work his way through—studying a few months and working a few months. He had spent much of his life hiking in the deserts around Tucson, so he thrived on this outdoor work of laying tracks and building bridges for the railroad. He was as tough and godless as you would expect anyone in such a crew to be, but he had a Christian uncle who took a deep interest in him.

One summer vacation Uncle John invited Arnett to join him in attending Camp Sychar near Mount Vernon, Ohio. Because he thought it was a summer youth camp where he might meet some pretty girls, Arnett gladly accepted the invitation. Imagine his shock when it turned out to be an old-fashioned Methodist "Holiness" camp meeting with three preaching services a day! But since Uncle John was helping to pay some of his expenses, Arnett felt he had to stay for at least a few days.

Along came Missionary Day, and Arnett reluctantly attended—sitting on one of the back seats. The special speaker, a well-known Methodist bishop from China, described the backwardness of the people and their need for Christ. The Bishop also talked of China's great need for roads and bridges and buildings—the very thing Arnett was specializing in. But by *now he was no longer listening to the speaker. He was daydreaming of going to China as an engineer and builder. He began to imagine making a name for himself and, of course, lots of money.*

Suddenly his daydream was rudely interrupted. A strange sensation— something, someone—seemed to be talking to him. But more than that, stretching across the top of the platform above the speaker's head there appeared a vision. One word was spelled out in fiery, silver letters: INDIA. An inner-voice, which was crystal-clear—as clear as the sign—was saying, "No, not China. I want you to be a missionary in India." It was all over in a matter of seconds, but it left Arnett physically and emotionally shaken—shaken with fear, but mostly anger. "How dare You (yes, of course, it was God—he knew that instinctively) interfere with my plans? A missionary to India? I'm not even a Christian!" He was so shaken he got up and left the meeting.

That's quite a story, isn't it? That young man was my dad, who was converted *after* his call to service. In spite of the strong advice that most Christians gave him, he did not quit engineering school and go to seminary. Instead, he stuck to his dream and finished his civil engineering degree. He said he "could not be disobedient to that heavenly vision." He held onto it, or rather it held onto him, even when he graduated first in his class and was called a fool by the Dean for turning down the envied prize—a scholarship to Cornell and the guarantee of a lucrative job. And he did become an "Engineer-Evangelist" missionary to India, serving there for more than forty years. He led thousands to Christ and built over 100 churches as well as hospitals and schools. In 1956, at the centennial celebration of Methodism in India, E. A. Seamands was named "Missionary of the Century" for the South India area.

Dad could never get away from the vision. After his official retirement in 1957, he returned six times to serve three-month terms in India. In 1978, he received a pacemaker for his failing heart and then went back six *more* times for some of the most productive years of his life. In 1984, at the age of ninety-two, he took his last trip to India and died there. We felt it most appropriate that he be buried in India where he lived out that glorious, God-given dream/vision.

I've listed for you a number of the results that stemmed from my father's initial dream/vision. The Seamands Tribe—I mean the Christian one—began when a vision turned my father around 180 degrees. Now you can understand why dreams and visions have always fascinated me.

Dreams are very important to my brother, to our children, and our grandchildren as well.

Do You Have a Dream?

God may not work that dramatically in everyone's life, but I believe He wants to give to all of His redeemed children some kind of a dream and vision which will hold them steadily on His intended course for their lives.

Many years ago, a young university student in England was asked to go to India and fill a job for just one year. This seemed to be an interesting possibility, so he accepted the offer. While he was there, he felt challenged by the work, and the dream of a lifetime of service began to fill his mind.

To make a long story short, Lesslie Newbigin became one of South India's most prominent evangelical missionaries. His books on missions and theology are classics. Newbigin had such an outstanding record that when several denominations united to form the indigenous Church of South India, he was one of the very few missionaries to be elected Bishop.

Let's make it personal. Do you have a dream? Have you ever had one? Perhaps we should ask if you still have the dream you once had—that high and holy vision for your life? A godly picture of who God intends you to be which propels you toward the goal? Which compels you, like the athletes we mentioned, to give your all? A dream like this is a form of sanctified imagination, holding before us an inner video of all we're meant to be.

> *Every Christian ought to be an imagineer for God.*

Richard Baxter, the great Puritan divine, had a way with words. He took two common words, *imagination* and *engineer,* and said that every Christian ought to be an *imagineer* for God. Such a dream gives us an inner power, a force which drives us, as Paul said, to "press on to take hold of that for which Christ Jesus took hold of me .... press on toward the goal to win the prize for which God has called me heavenward in Christ Jesus" (Philippians 3:12-14).

Paul's great dream came not when he was asleep, but when he was wide awake in broad daylight. He had been filled with a dream—a terrible, murderous dream of going to Damascus to ferret out Christians and put them into prison. Before he reached his destination, Christ appeared to him and gave him a new dream (Acts 9:11-18; 26:12-18). Paul called it a "vision" and said he had never been "disobedient to the vision from heaven" (Acts 26:19). It became the guiding goal of his life. Literally, in spite of hell and high water (Acts 19:13-20; 27:27-44), he never stopped pursuing it. It gave him a great inner sense of purpose and self-confidence. "I can do everything through Him who gives me strength" (Philippians 4:13).

In His Parable of the Talents (Matthew 25:14-28), Jesus did not praise the fearful man who never had enough vision or confidence to risk using his single talent. Rather, He praised those who had the sanctified imagination and self-assurance to use theirs. He rewarded them by increasing the talents they did have.

I've always appreciated a story which is told about President Teddy Roosevelt, a man of considerable self-assurance. You may not know that he was a very good singer. He had a deep, resonant voice and loved to use it. One day he was telling friends how much he was looking forward to heaven, because he envisioned a great choir singing there. "Why," said he, "in my mind's eye I can picture it. There will be 10,000 sopranos," and he named some of the great sopranos of his day. "And 10,000 altos and 10,000 tenors," and once again he named some of the day's greatest singers. "It's going to be tremendous."

"But Mr. President," someone asked, "what about the basses?" "Oh," said he with a laugh, "*I'm* going to sing bass!"

Dreams Developing

God wants to give us a dream, a vision, a high and holy picture of His intention for our lives—just as He did for Joseph. As we take a close look at Joseph's life, we'll first consider some of the factors that went into building those dreams. Later we'll see how and why those dreams got into trouble.

I already mentioned that the chapter sequence in Genesis does not follow the exact historical sequence. There is a lot of moving back and forth; interesting incidents of history are interspersed with sections that begin with "This is the account of Esau" (Genesis 36:1) or "This is the account of Jacob" (Genesis 37:2). There is also a lot of literal moving around by Jacob and his family. His sons Simeon and Levi went to such outlandish extremes of pillage and murder to avenge the sexual violation of their sister Dinah, that Jacob had to move away from Shechem (Genesis 34). The family went back for a brief time to Bethel. Then, as they were moving from there, Rachel, Joseph's mother, died while giving birth to his younger brother Benjamin (Genesis 35:16-20). Once again they moved, at least partly because of the scandal caused by Reuben's incestuous behavior with one of Jacob's concubines (Genesis 35:22, 27). This time they settled back in Canaan (Hebron) somewhere near Isaac, Jacob's father. Although Genesis 35:28-29 tells of Isaac's death and burial, in reality this did not happen until many years later.

When we put it all together, on the basis of the years and ages given in Genesis, most Bible scholars agree on this approximate chronology. Jacob was 97 years old when he returned home and Isaac was 157. At that time Joseph was only 6 years old. When our story opens, he was a youth of 17, Jacob was 108, and Isaac was 168. Isaac died at the age of 180, so he must have still been living at Hebron for 12 years after Joseph had been sold into slavery by his brothers. This means that Joseph lost his mother when he was around 12 and after that lived for at least 5 years in the neighborhood of his grandfather, Isaac.

> *God wants to give us a dream, a vision, a high and holy picture of His intention for our lives.*

Why these details? Because I think Grandpa Isaac played an important role in Joseph's spiritual development. Often in my pastoral experience I have seen grandparents going out of their way to give special attention and affection to a grandchild who has lost a parent. It would be very natural for Grandpa Isaac to take under his wing, and into his heart, this motherless teenager who was Jacob's favorite son and the recognized heir of the birthright. It may have begun as a ministry of comfort to a young lad who had lost his mother, but God intended it for something far deeper. It's not hard to imagine Joseph sitting at the feet of blind old Isaac, listening in rapt attention to his grandfather's wonderful stories. I'm sure one was his special favorite.

"Grandpa, tell me that one again."

"But Son, I've told it so many times before."

"I know, but I want to hear it again—please."

And so Isaac would recount the story of that incredible three-day journey during his own boyhood with his father, Abraham. He would draw out the details of that mysterious climb up Mount Moriah and then dramatize the terror of those traumatic moments. Lifting his right hand into the air as if he were holding the knife of sacrifice, he would bring it down swiftly toward his own heart. At the last second, he would grab that wrist with his other hand, just as the angel had stopped Abraham's hand (Genesis 22). Through this relationship, I believe God was beginning to show Joseph his covenant heritage—a wonderful sense of where he had come from, who he really was, and who God wanted him to be. A deep inner sense of identity began to develop within young Joseph. It was the beginning of his noble aspirations, the vision that would shape his life. I believe wise and godly influences prepared him for his dreams.

But there were also some unwise and ungodly ingredients which would play a part in the early shattering of those dreams. These began with Jacob, who was thoughtless in the way he showed his favoritism of his son Joseph. Parental sins tend to repeat themselves in children—generational sins, we call them. You would have thought Jacob's memories of the havoc wrought by the sin of his parents' favoritism would have made him hesitate. It had disrupted his parents' marriage, driven his mother to treachery and deceit, and had produced a long-lasting and almost fatal enmity between Jacob and his brother, Esau. (Genesis 25 and Genesis 32).

Jacob did not seem to learn from the sins of his own family's favoritism. Instead, he repeated them by openly showing his special love and preference for Joseph. He foolishly appointed him to keep an eye on his older half-brothers, and soon Joseph was bringing bad reports about their work. In addition, we are told that Jacob "loved Joseph more than any of his other sons, because he had been born to him in his old age; and [Jacob] made a richly ornamented robe for him" (Genesis 37:3). This added insult to injury, for in those days this distinctive type of dress was not only a sign of favoritism, but also signified the one who was heir to the father's inheritance. It is no wonder that "when his brothers saw that their father loved him more than any of them, they hated him and could not speak a kind word to him" (Genesis 37:4). Remember, all this took place prior to the dream incident. Long before Joseph told his brothers about his dreams, Jacob had senselessly set him up to be the object of their jealousy and hatred.

Yes, generational sins tend to repeat themselves in amazing fashion. I remember a gospel song, "Will the Circle Be Unbroken?" which was sometimes sung at funerals when I was a youngster. The question that often comes to me now in my family counseling ministry is quite the opposite—"Will the cycle ever be broken?" That is, the vicious cycle of family sin which so often tends to repeat itself in succeeding generations.

We see this vividly in Jacob's life at a much later date in the Joseph saga.

In Genesis 48, there is a detailed description of how Joseph brought
Manasseh and Ephraim, his two sons, to be blessed by the aging Jacob.
As they knelt before their grandfather, Joseph had deliberately placed
Manasseh, the elder son, so that Jacob's right hand would be laid on his
head to give him the chief blessing. In spite of Joseph's displeasure and
protest, Jacob deliberately crossed his arms and reversed the blessing so
that it fell on Ephraim, the younger son (Genesis 48:12-20). In this way,
Jacob repeated what he and his crafty, doting mother had tricked Isaac
into doing a generation before.

The Bible has always shown generational sins to be tenacious and their
hold hard to break. In recent years, the behavioral sciences have finally
caught up with Scripture and began exploring *dysfunctional families*.
Research has called our attention to the destructive results in the children
of such families. For example, a large percentage of children from alcoholic
families either become alcoholics themselves or end up marrying alcoholics. A surprising number who divorce one alcoholic spouse will then marry
another. Children who have been abused often grow up to be abusers. This
is why all kinds of support groups have been formed to help break such
vicious cycles.

In my previous books, I have dealt with the healing and "reprogramming", or relearning, necessary to break out of such generational sins. Here
I want to emphasize that the sinful power of such destructive, compulsive
patterns from the past must be faced with ruthless moral honesty and
dealt with, in spite of the pain this will bring. They will not go away if we
ignore them, and they won't be outgrown simply by the passing of time.
Furthermore, they are not automatically taken care of by the miracle of
conversion, or by some deeper experience of the Holy Spirit. Remember, it
had been many years since Jacob's face-to-face, life-transforming encoun-
ters with God at Peniel and Bethel. He had been given a new name, Israel,
and a new nature which certainly affected his spirit in significant ways—
but many of those destructive family traits remained.

After dealing with Christians for many years, I am convinced that such
problems often require a special kind of emotional and spiritual healing
plus a long-term commitment to a process of being transformed by the
renewing of the mind (Romans 12:2). Unfortunately, too many Christians
look for some quickie cure. They simply will not pay the price necessary to
really change their thinking and their behavior.

Broken Dreams

The tragedy is that generational sins can so quickly damage or destroy our God-given dreams. This is especially true of the dreams we have for our marriages, as shown by the following example.

Jim was a young man who called rather hesitantly to make an appointment for "some marriage counseling for Claire and me." I had attended their wedding several years earlier and remembered it vividly. Now they sat together on a couch before me. Claire was obviously embarrassed and reached for a Kleenex before we got started. She motioned for Jim to speak. He started by telling me all the good things, wanting to make sure I didn't get any wrong ideas. "I love Claire. She's a wonderful woman—I mean a really deep Christian too. She puts me to shame with her devotional life and her work for the church. She's a loving wife; our sex life—when we have it—couldn't be better." On and on it went.

I've learned to listen without comment to this kind of recital as it is usually the prelude to the problem. Finally, the discord was sounded—Claire's seemingly uncontrollable temper which, like a sudden storm, could strike out of nowhere and leave a path of destruction in its wake. And when I say "strike," that was what Claire literally did— both verbally and physically.

It happened for the first time a few days after their honeymoon. It was a terrible shock to both of them, and they cried and prayed together about it; however, the incidents continued—not often, but often enough to put shadows on their marital dreams. Now they were expecting a baby, and both of them were scared of what might happen with their child. Claire had to face the truth about her own family, where there had been a pattern of verbal abuse and occasional physical violence—especially on the part of her mother.

The amazing part of their story was that during a fairly lengthy courtship, there had never been any indication of this problem. However, while attending a seminar for engaged couples, they had been given the Taylor Johnson Temperament Analysis (TJTA). Everything looked quite normal, except that Claire's hostility was shown to be very high. Jim and Claire had talked about this, and she shared the family problem with Jim—but told him she hated it so much she was sure she could never be like that! This is perhaps the most deceptive thing about such problems. We think that because we grew up hating these family characteristics and telling ourselves, *I'll never be like that*, we are rid of them. Basically, we deny these characteristics and push them out of our minds. Often they go deeper into our personalities, fastening themselves onto our unexpressed frustration and rage. Unknown to us, they become a part of our own actions and reactions. Then one day, when we try to form intimate relationships, they explode with the force of a volcano, destroying our dreams with their molten lava.

Even if your specific problem is quite different, you may have been identifying with Joe and Claire. Let me say to you what I said to them after assuring them that I was willing to work with them in what could be a rather long-term healing process: "You need to choose your pain. In some ways it could be easier for you to limp along as you have been, choosing to bear your present pain. At least you know it, and in that sense you are comfortable with it. Or, you can choose a different kind of pain— the pain of confronting the truth about yourself and your family. Confront the pain:

- The pain of not excusing or rationalizing or blaming someone else
- The pain of never again saying, 'If only' or 'I can't help it; it's a family trait' or 'It's just the way I am'
- The pain of learning new and constructive ways of handling disappointment and frustration
- The pain of learning how to 'speak the truth in love'

You're in pain now; for a time you'll be in pain again, but it will be a productive pain like that of surgery and recuperation which leads to wholeness. Yes, you need to choose your pain."

> *It is only the healing and reprogramming power of the Holy Spirit that can truly free us from these chains which bind us to the nightmares of the past.*

By the grace of God they chose the right pain, so that healing and joy and harmonious love increasingly became the pattern of their marriage. No—not perfect, but good enough to maintain stability even when their child was in the throes of "the terrible two's."

I have heard this kind of story many times. It can involve everything from rage, verbal abuse, lust, and violence to compulsive and addictive behaviors. Except when God chooses to provide a single healing cure—a miracle—there are no emotional or spiritual shortcuts to dealing with generational problems of this nature. A great deal of honesty, courage, and spiritual determination are required by those caught in the web—a complex tangle of the sins of others, intermingled with their own. They often need the help of a pastor, counselor, or group who will join with them in commitment to provide the support and intercessory prayer necessary to bring about genuine change. They must always accept personal responsibility and the hard work that goes along with it.

It is only the healing and reprogramming power of the Holy Spirit that can truly free us from these chains which bind us to the nightmares of the past. If we choose our own power, we are on the road to broken dreams. Such was the situation with Joseph, as a result of Jacob's failure to break with his family sins.

Immature Dreams

There was one more factor—Joseph's dreams—which helped pave the way for the disaster at Dothan. Let us remind ourselves of the details of the story as we find them in Genesis 37:5-11. "We were binding sheaves of grain out in the field when suddenly my sheaf rose and stood upright, while your sheaves gathered around mine and bowed down to it." When Joseph told this dream to his brothers, they were furious because the meaning was so obvious. Indignantly they asked, "Do you intend to reign over us? Will you actually rule us?" No wonder the author of Genesis adds, "And they hated him all the more because of his dream and what he had said."

But the worst was yet to come. Sometime later he had another dream, which he again promptly told to his brothers. "Listen," he said, "I had another dream and this time the sun and moon and eleven stars were bowing down to me." The eleven stars so unmistakably referred to his eleven brothers that even his father was shocked and scolded him severely. "What is this dream you had? Will your mother and I and your brothers actually come and bow down to the ground before you?" Again, it's no surprise that the author comments, "His brothers were jealous of him," and then adds, "but his father kept the matter in mind."

If Jacob's open favoritism had not already poisoned the brothers, filling them with envy and hatred for Joseph, maybe they would have taken an entirely different attitude toward Joseph's dreams. After all, they were much older than their kid brother. They could have just laughed at such outlandish dreams, passing them off as the crazy fantasies of their imaginative brother. However, like paranoids who are convinced that everything everyone does is just one more proof that they're "out to get them," they thought Joseph was rubbing it in. Consequently, they "hated him all the more for his dream and for what he had said." We have to conclude that

Joseph was extremely unwise and immature in the way he shared his dreams with the very people he saw as subservient to him.

Here is a good lesson for all of us. Certainly God can plant dreams in our minds, both when we are asleep and when we're awake. He had done this for Joseph, but those dreams needed to be tested by silence and tempered by time. The way Joseph described the dreams, his brothers got the impression he expected them to bow down and obey him right away. Naturally, this infuriated them. What was Joseph's hurry? His dreams obviously had to wait in order to be fulfilled, so he should have waited before he expressed them so openly.

We all need to learn that there is an important time factor to our dreams and visions. Even after we make sure they really have come from God, we must also make sure we are on God's timetable. Both the dreams and their schedule need to come from Him. This is why the vision God gives for our lives often needs the discipline of darkness and the delay of a detour. As fallen creatures, we are infected with pride, self-centeredness, and also with a tendency to be in a hurry. Many older translations render the last part of Isaiah 28:16: "He that believeth shall not make haste" (*KJV*).

Even the most mature Christians can get caught in their own urgency. One day a parishioner entered the office of Joseph Parker, the great New England preacher, and found him pacing back

"The problem is I'm in a hurry, but God isn't!"

and forth, hands clasped tightly behind his back. "Dr. Parker," he asked, "what's the problem?"

The preacher replied, "The problem is I'm in a hurry, but God isn't!"

There is one more aspect of Joseph's dreams which God had to change and deepen considerably. Joseph needed far more than the rewards that filled those early dreams—the achievement of status, position, and authority with his brothers and family members bowing down before him. God would deepen his dreams so they included not only accomplishments but *relationships*. We see this so clearly in the later chapters of his life as his dreams were being fulfilled and the "eleven stars" were bowing down before him. That was no longer enough for Joseph. By then he needed them not just as subjects and servants, but as brothers and family.

When young Christians share their dreams with me, they often say something to the effect that they "want to do great things for God." They don't want to be "ordinary," to be "just one more"—whatever it is. I appreciate the spirit behind this, but I also sense the danger. They envision

themselves largely in the realm of achievements and accomplishments—
doing—whereas God wants to refine those dreams so that they are bal-
anced with the *being* which comes through relationships—both with God
and with other people. Jesus said to His disciples, "I no longer call you
servants... [but] friends" (John 15:15). Joseph needed to have both the
intent and the content of his dreams deepened by the maturity that only
time and testing could bring.

Let me share something with those of you who are young in years or in
the faith—something that has been one of my most painful experiences of
growing older. As I look back on many of the accomplishments I once
considered among the best in my service for God, I am often shocked as
the Spirit reveals to me how mixed my motives were. There was far more of
"self" in them than I was aware of at the time, far more desire to accomplish speedy results than to achieve satisfactory relationships. Again and
again God refined those motives by allowing me to go through some
painful experiences. Isn't this what He is trying to tell us through His
Word?

> When all kinds of trials and temptations crowd into your lives, my
> brothers, don't resent them as intruders, but welcome them as friends!
> Realize they come to test your faith and to produce in you the quality
> of endurance. But let the process go on until that endurance is fully
> developed, and you will find you have become men of mature charac-
> ter, men of integrity with no weak spots (James 1:2-4, *PH*).

Joseph's dreams needed the test of time and maturity. They needed
refining, honing, and polishing. God did not tamper with the dreams, but
He did temper the dreamer. He did not remove the dreams, but He did
refine both the dreams and the dreamer. Just as God was in the dreams, so
God was with Joseph in every step of the refining process. This is a truth
we must never forget. It's a good thing Joseph didn't forget, for his dreams
were about to go down the drain at Dothan.

3

DESTROYERS OF
THE DREAM

Don Wildmon was the pastor of a United Methodist church in a small town in Mississippi. A dedicated and godly man, he faithfully served the people of his congregation. One cold night in December 1976, he sat down with his wife and four children to enjoy watching television together. He had anticipated an evening of family fun and entertainment. Instead, he was shocked to find that the only programs on all three of the major networks featured promiscuous sex, crude profanity, and graphic violence. He became alarmed and concerned. After doing considerable research, Don preached a sermon about it in early 1977. But he did more than that. He challenged his people to "go cold turkey" by observing a "Turn the TV Off Week" in late February. This event was preceded by a phone and letter-writing campaign to all the newspapers, radio and TV stations of the Memphis area. To his utter astonishment, the whole matter got picked up by the Associated Press, and within days, thousands of letters and phone calls started coming in from all over the country! It was then that God implanted in Don Wildmon a dream: to leave the pastorate and give his time to founding and directing an organization: The National Federation for Decency.

For an unknown man, with no money and with a family to support, to take on the awesome power of the networks—that was a dream, all right, a crazy dream! But his organization and its later affiliates won a major battle against Sears Roebuck in 1978. By 1988 the foundation had forced the networks to cancel several major programs and caused Universal Studios to lose millions from The Last Temptation of Christ. At this point, the country recognized that a God-given, high and holy dream was at work.

This sinful world hates any dream or dreamer who interferes with its evil ways

Don Wildmon is now Executive Director of both the American Family Association and CLEAR TV (Christian Leaders for Responsible Television), which includes a network of representatives from almost every denomination in the USA. The story of that dream is told in an exciting book, *Don Wildmon, The Man the Networks Love To Hate.*[1] It reads like a modern version of the story of David and Goliath!

As long as Don Wildmon served God in a small pastorate, it didn't matter to very many people what he dreamed or envisioned. *But when living out his dreams took him into enemy territory, then all hell broke loose.* This fallen and sinful world hates any dream or dreamer who interferes with its evil ways, and it will do all it can to destroy both dream and dreamer.

This is unmistakably illustrated in the life of Joseph. One day his father sent him to check up on his brothers who were grazing the flocks near Shechem. "Go and see if all is well with your brothers and with the flocks, and bring word back to me" (Genesis 37:14). Shechem, located in a very fertile valley, was well over a two-day trip north from Hebron. It was there that the bloody encounter had taken place between the Shechemites and Jacob's sons over the sexual violation of their sister, Dinah (Genesis 34). Jacob had a right to be worried about a possible flare-up of this feud, and so he sent Joseph to see if his brothers were all right.

But when Joseph arrived at Shechem, he was told that his brothers and the flocks had moved on to Dothan; so he made the additional journey of thirteen miles to find them. Since this was all flat pastureland, and since Joseph was wearing his ornamental coat, the brothers saw him from quite a distance. "Here comes that dreamer!" they said, and immediately plotted to kill him, throw his body into a dry cistern, and then tell everyone that some ferocious animal had attacked him. "Then we'll see what comes of his dreams," they added exultantly (Genesis 37:19). The vote was ten to one, which shows just how much they really did hate him. Reuben begged them not to shed blood—after all Joseph was their half-brother—but to throw him in the cistern and leave him there. Actually, Reuben planned to return later, rescue him, and take him back to their father (Genesis 37:22).

The brothers, not knowing Reuben's secret intent, agreed on the revised plan, for it would rid them of Joseph without actually having to kill him. The record sounds as unemotional as a police report. "So when Joseph came to his brothers, they stripped him of his robe—the richly ornamented robe he was wearing—and they took him and threw him into the cistern. Now the cistern was empty; there was no water in it ... they sat down to eat their meal..." (Genesis 37:23-25).

This cistern was the kind dug by shepherds to store water during the rainy season so that they would have an adequate supply for their flocks. The cistern was shaped like a bottle or vase, with a narrow mouth so that a single flat stone could cover it; inside it widened to form a large subterranean room. It was terrible to be thrown into one of those underground tanks, because there was no escape without assistance from someone at the top. We can imagine what a terrifying experience it was for Joseph. Years later, when the brothers were confessing the guilt of their dastardly deed they said, "Surely we are being punished because of our brother. *We saw how distressed he was when he pleaded with us for his life, but we would not listen"* (Genesis 42:21, italics mine) We can almost hear the agonizing screams of Joseph echoing back and forth from the cavernous chamber of death. Such heartless cruelty is nearly beyond imagination, for while he begged and pleaded for his life, the brothers sat nearby and ate their meal. Hundreds of years later, when the prophet Amos was looking for some way to describe the indifference of his hardhearted generation, he cried out against them. "Woe to them...that drink wine in bowls, and anoint themselves with the chief ointments; but they are not grieved for the affliction of Joseph" (Amos 6:1,6, *KJV*).

What better illustration of just how much the world really does hate the dreams of God's people! The Revised Standard Version translates *cistern* as "pit." I remind you that all the forces of Satan and evil stand ready to throw us together with our godly aspirations into a pit. There are many pits and many pitfalls we will face when we start out to reach the goal. Isaac Watts, in his great hymn, "Am I a Soldier of the Cross?" brings out this truth so forcefully by a series of questions:

> Am I a soldier of the cross,
> A follower of the Lamb,
> And shall I fear to own His cause
> Or blush to speak His name?
>
> Are there no foes for me to face?
> Must I not stem the flood?
> Is this vile world a friend to grace,
> To help me on to God?

Everyone knows the answer to the last question. This vile world is not a friend to grace and will not help us on to God. The world actually resents anyone with a high and holy dream and will do all in its power to deflect us from our goal.

Where was Joseph's dream now? It seemed to have gone down the drain at Dothan. It appeared that the dream had ended before it could even get started, and it all happened so quickly. Most of us have had similar experiences. We start out with a shiny idea that we feel has come from God, and within a short time, something or someone has put a damper of opposition on it or has dumped it—or us—into a pit. From the bright sunshine of our dreams and visions we seem to have been suddenly thrown into the darkness of a dungeon. We literally feel down in the dumps!

Our Personal Dothan

Shortly after my conversion as a teenager, I began to feel called to go as a missionary to India where I had grown up. In contrast to my father's visionlike call, mine was a gradual process. The inner conviction and feeling that this was God's will for my life grew increasingly stronger until it filled my horizons. During my college days, my dream began to take shape. It was a God-given vision from which I never once deviated, and it brought a deep peace and certainty to my life.

During those days at Asbury College, God brought Helen and me together. We had much in common: we were the youngest members of our class, were both Methodist preachers'/missionaries' kids, and shared the same crazy sense of humor. Best of all, God had also implanted in her a missionary dream. Everyone joined in our happiness when, after a fairly lengthy courtship, we decided to get married. Both sets of parents insisted we wait until after finishing college. We graduated at noon and were married at four!

After completing seminary and graduate work, Helen and I, with our year-old daughter Sharon, set sail for India and arrived in July 1946. We were appointed to the specific location and the exact type of work for which we had been preparing. It was exciting—the dreams we had envisioned so long were finally being fulfilled! But my energy level began to drop and I kept slowly losing weight, something my 135-pound body could not afford to do. It turned out that I had picked up amoebic dysentery almost upon our arrival. The next months were an up-and-downhill battle just to stay strong enough to continue language study and do some evangelistic work in the villages.

In May 1947, David Jr. was born—our first son and the first grandson. By this time my health was better; I had passed the first Kanarese language exam and even preached a sermon in it. One morning when little Davey was a healthy nine-month-old, Helen shared with me a terrible dream she had had. She dreamed that Davey had died and we were burying him. She was deeply troubled by the emotions of her dream. I tried to be sympathetic, but my skepticism was a bit too obvious.

Two weeks later, I was to go on an evangelistic tour in the villages. Still remembering the dream, Helen pleaded with me not to go. In my concern for my work, I ignored her emotional appeal in favor of my much more rational approach. When I kissed Davey good-bye, he was a healthy, happy baby; but by the very next night, I had received the mission doctor's desperate message telling me to return home at once. Davey was very ill. The doctor called it "fulminant bacillary dysentery." *Fulminant* comes from a Latin word which means "to strike with lightning." That was certainly an appropriate name, for by noon the next day we had buried our beloved son in the tiny cemetery on the mission compound in Bidar.

Unfortunately, the dream—more like a nightmare—had come true. You can be sure that since then I have had a high regard for Helen's intuitive knowledge and spiritual perceptions. We now realize that God was, in some mysterious and loving way, trying to prepare us for the tragedy. My parents were stationed only 100 miles away, but by the time they got our message that Davey was in danger and drove over, it was late that night. They hurried out of their Jeep and started toward the back steps of our house. Mother anxiously asked, "How's little Davey?"

I replied, "I'm sorry to tell you, Mom, but we buried him this morning."

By then they were on the steps. My dad was one of the most saintly men I ever knew. He literally "practiced the presence" of God and talked with Him at any time—just like one would talk to a close friend. Dad stopped on the top step, and looked up into the starlit sky. There was a long silence. Finally, with just the slightest edge to his voice, he said, "Father, I don't understand this!" And he walked on into the house.

We didn't understand either, certainly not at the time. It seemed like a great many of our dreams had been smashed and dashed within such a short time. And of course, though we didn't know it then, we were soon going to be caught up in the seething turmoil of the early days of Indian independence, and many more of our dreams would have to be refashioned. It was going to take awhile before we could actually see how God was going to work out the dreams He had given us. At that time, down in the dumps of our "Dothan", we did not understand.

> *Youthful dreams are not sufficient to overcome the world. We must learn humility and total dependence on God's power.*

We can be sure that Joseph, crying out from that cistern, didn't understand. Perhaps you don't either. One thing we do learn early in life is that those high and holy goals are not as easily reached as we had thought. People do not respond to them as we had hoped. God doesn't seem to bring them to pass as we had planned and prayed. The best youthful dreams, plus the energy and confidence they bring, are not sufficient to overcome the world. We must learn humility and total dependence on God's power, and we can learn these things only by walking the way of adversity and difficulty. It didn't look as if Joseph was even going to *live* long enough to have the chance to learn. But wait...Joseph's story is not over. It's really only just beginning.

God Engineers Our Circumstances

Years ago, before the days of the automobile, there was a minister who, although retired, still loved to preach. One week he received two invitations for the same Sunday morning. He wanted to accept both of the invitations and discovered, to his great joy, that he could because of the timing of the two services. One was an early service at nine o'clock and the other at eleven. However, he would have to catch the ferry to cross the river, which separated the two sections of the town in which the churches were located.

He timed it perfectly. Finishing the first service a little early, he walked down toward the river as fast as he could to catch the 10:30 ferry. Alas, as he rounded the corner he looked down and saw he had missed it. In fact, the boat was just leaving the dock and was only a few feet or so out in the water. He shouted to the people on deck, and taking a flying leap he jumped—and landed safely on the deck of the ferry. His momentum propelled him into the arms of a big, burly man who caught him and held him there as he puffed and panted breathlessly. Then the man looked at him and asked in a disgusted tone, "What in the world are you doing? This boat's not going out. It's just coming in!"

So it is with Joseph. His boat is really just coming in—only with him it's a ship of the desert: a camel. God is going to make all this part of His plan and His schedule. There is more at work here than just the forces of evil which we can see so plainly. God has never been more involved in Joseph's life than at this time. Oswald Chambers, the great devotional writer, calls God the "Engineer of our circumstances." It is a constant theme in his writings.

> One of the last things we learn is that God engineers our circumstances; we do not believe He does, we say we do. Never look for second causes, if you do you will go wrong. We blunder when we look at circumstances as secondary.[2]

> That God engineers our circumstances for us if we accept His purpose in Christ is a thought of great practical moment.[3]

We can watch the great Engineer at work at Dothan. "As they sat down to eat their meal, they looked up and saw a caravan of Ishmaelites coming from Gilead. Their camels were loaded with spices, balm and myrrh, and they were on their way to take them down to Egypt" (Genesis 37:25). If we could only remember—for every pit of Satan, God has a caravan on the way! Joseph's dream had been interrupted and turned into a nightmare. Now God interrupts the interruption with a caravan of Ishmaelites (also known as Midianites), foreign merchants on a string of camels going to Egypt. What an interesting twist the Lord of History put on this! The great-grandsons of Ishmael and Midian, both Abraham's sons (Genesis 25:2), have come along to rescue Joseph, the great-grandson of Abraham. How is God going to work all this out to fit His purposes?

As Paul Harvey would put it, "Now let me tell you the rest of the story." Judah—strange, his name sounds so much like Judas—thought of an even better

> *For every pit of Satan, God has a caravan on the way!*

plan. Why not get rid of Joseph and make some money at the same time? In this instance, the vote was unanimous since Reuben wasn't there to protest. The brothers pulled Joseph up out of the cistern and sold him to the traders for twenty pieces of silver, the average price for a male slave in those days (Genesis 37:26-28). Of course, when Reuben returned and saw that his secret plan to rescue Joseph had been thwarted, he was terribly upset. But the evil eleven soon thought of a perfect cover-up. They took Joseph's special robe, smeared it with the blood of a goat, carried it back to their father, and said with deceitful innocence, "We found this. Examine it to see whether it is your son's robe." In the very way they put the question, "your son," not "our brother," they disowned their kinship to Joseph and any responsibility for his death. Jacob, of course, was inconsolably grieved by the death of his favorite son. He simply refused to be comforted—not too surprising when you consider who his comforters were (Genesis 37:29-35).

Meanwhile, the Midianites took Joseph to Egypt and sold him to Potiphar, one of Pharaoh's officials, the captain of the guard (Genesis 37:36).

"But why Egypt?" someone asks, "I don't understand it."

Of course not. We don't, but He does. God wanted the family of Israel relocated to Egypt for a few hundred years. Why? Wasn't Canaan promised to be their land? Yes, it was indeed; but Canaan was filled with warlike tribes. At that time there existed only a handful of Israelites. As long as they stayed just a small group, other tribes would have left them alone; but God needed them in great numbers. When their numbers began to grow, however, these tribes would have gotten alarmed and wiped them out. God's plan was to take them to a place where they could live peacefully and securely and grow into a large nation.

They also needed to be set apart, becoming separate from other pagan nations. They must become Israel, God's people, so that they could receive God's law, produce prophets, teachers, singers, writers, and ultimately bring forth the Messiah—the Redeemer of the entire world. If by chance the Canaanite tribes had allowed them to live in peace, the Israelites would have mingled with them and been absorbed by them. Instead, the children of Israel must be taken to a place where this would not happen. Egypt was the ideal place. The Egyptians were a proud and exclusive people who did not associate closely with foreigners (Genesis 43:32). In Goshen, then, protected and favored by Joseph, Jacob's family would be safe, segregated, and shut up to themselves.

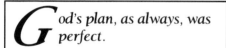

God's plan, as always, was perfect.

Furthermore, while the Canaanites were quite crude, barbaric, and without much learning, Egypt was the seat of one of the world's highest civilizations. The pyramids had already been built; there were libraries, universities, arts, culture, and all this would become a part of Israel's experience. It would make possible a Moses, a prince of the palace, who could ultimately lead God's people and write the Books of the Law.

God's plan, as always, was perfect. The seventeen-year-old youth who cried out in anguish as he was thrown into the cistern, and wept as he was rescued out of the frying pan only to be thrown into the fire of slavery, watching his dreams go down the drain—*he didn't know all this.* Those rough desert Bedouins plodding across the countryside on their camels—*they didn't know this.* Those hateful, cruel brothers gleefully pocketing their share of the silver pieces—*they didn't know this.* And a heartbroken father looking at that beautiful coat, now stained with what he thought was his son's blood, would moan and mourn for years to come—*he didn't know this.*

But *God knew.* Joseph didn't fully understand until years later, when he was able to say to his brothers, "It was not you who sent me here, but God" (Genesis 45:8).

Joseph had a dream. The dream got badly damaged at Dothan. What pulled Joseph through the next thirteen years of struggle and suffering? God. Yes, God and the dream he gave Joseph. Joseph had a dream. He would have never made it without one—and neither will any of us, either.

4

SEDUCERS OF
THE DREAM

It is Sunday night. Everyone is impatient for the mini-series to begin. It has been advertised for weeks in magazines, through T.V. commercials, spots on talk shows, and newspaper headlines. Based on a best-seller and featuring famous actors, the series has millions of viewers taking their phones off the hook in anticipation of The Amazing Saga of Joseph Jacobson, the Jewish immigrant lad who had made it to the top.

The first segment shows the youngster, Joey, growing up in a large, complicated, and dysfunctional family. There are many incidents depicting favoritism, conflict, and sibling rivalry. There is a scene in which his mother, after a long and painful labor, dies giving birth to his younger brother, Benji. When little Joey and his father kneel to give her a farewell kiss and to sob over their loss, millions of sympathetic women reach for a Kleenex. After that the plot thickens. Joe, now a bright and appealing youth of seventeen, is shown being cruelly mistreated by his jealous brothers. They start out to kill him, but instead, they end up selling him to a traveling gang of wicked men who plan to take him to Egypt and sell him as a slave. The episode ends with the youth in chains, sitting on top of a camel, weeping silently as the long caravan plods into the sunset.

After the last commercials, there are previews of the next episode. One of them shows a scantily clad, strikingly beautiful woman in her bedroom. She is obviously attempting to seduce our hero, Joseph—now a grown man, muscular and handsome. The scene fades just as she is reaching toward him. Millions of viewers determine not to miss the next installment, not even for Monday night football.

Monday night's episode begins at the Egyptian slave market. Because of Joe's rugged physique and exceptional good looks, the bidding goes high. He is finally sold to Captain Potiphar, a high official in Pharaoh's Palace Guard. From there the dazed youth is led up a pillared avenue through *gates guarded by massive stone sphinxes. All around him he hears a strange language, and he feels very much like the alien that he is.*

Then the scene changes to a few years later. Joseph has learned the language and mastered the peculiar customs of Egypt. The viewers watch him being promoted to higher and higher positions in Potiphar's household. Even though he is a foreigner, again and again the name of Joseph Jacobson is brought up whenever someone of integrity is needed. He proves to be fully trustworthy—a rare quality amidst the thievery and scandals of the household. Finally, several years later there is a moving episode showing him being warmly installed by Captain Potiphar as the overseer of all the household servants and affairs. The Captain is often gone because of his special duties in Pharaoh's Bodyguard, and he needs someone he can trust completely.

Ah, then comes the part millions have been waiting for. On the pretext of needing something, Mrs. Potiphar calls Joseph into her private chambers. Her face and eyes have been made up to perfection. The very way she speaks his name gives a hint, and her costume leaves no doubt of what she has in mind. She is dressed in a sheer silken robe under which the outline of her voluptuous body is plainly visible. Joseph looks away, but she comes closer and forces him to face her.

Of course, at this point the music changes. Excitement builds, for everyone recognizes the prelude to a sexual encounter. She invites Joe to go to bed with her, but he refuses, saying he cannot betray the Captain who trusts him implicitly. He leaves as quickly as possible.

The viewers are disappointed, but are soon relieved when the scene is repeated again and again. Her costumes become more revealing and her entreaties more desperate, but Joseph continues to refuse. Finally, he will not even come when she calls. He cannot betray his master's trust, and he will not sin against his God. It is then that the awful truth dawns on the millions of viewers. This guy is not going to bed with her. He's going to keep turning her down. There is just not going to be any affair or sexy bed scenes in this mini-series! *All over the nation millions of viewers angrily turn off their TVs or switch channels to watch football.*

For the next twenty-four hours, phone lines to every affiliate of the network are jammed. The sponsors are furious. The ratings reveal that only a handful of people tune in to the final episode. The others never see how Joseph Jacobson makes it to the highest office in the land.

By now you know this account is a figment of my imagination. Such a story should inspire us, but frequently it doesn't. It just bores us, and yet it is a story we desperately need to hear. How did Joseph do it? How did he stay pure?

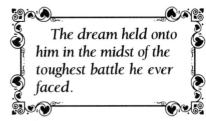

The dream held onto him in the midst of the toughest battle he ever faced.

What kept him from slipping into the pit of seduction? A dream—a high, holy, godly dream for his life. His dream included a vision of sexual purity, and he held onto that dream. Perhaps we might even say that *the dream held onto him in the midst of the toughest battle he ever faced.* The most remarkable thing about this incident is that although everything was against Joseph, he still came through without yielding.

Let's look at the factors which would have made it so easy for Joseph to fall. By relating them to our own contemporary situations, we can hear God's Word to us through them.

"Everybody's Doing It!"

The findings of archeology tell us that Egyptian women of Joseph's day enjoyed considerable freedom. This, combined with moral laxity, led to sexual promiscuity. The decadence of Pharaoh's court compares remarkably to the scandals of Washington's official circles today. When immorality is rampant at the top, it soon filters down. It could be said then as now, "Everybody's doing it." Joseph had to swim against the moral tide of his times, as do Christians today who want to maintain their vision of holy sexuality.

Some time ago I watched a stand-up comedian do a spot on an otherwise decent TV special. It was a monologue of a preacher performing a wedding ceremony. "Dearly beloved," he intoned, "we are gathered together here to join this man and woman together in holy matrimony, so that we can now make legal what they have been doing together for the last four years. We give sanction and approval, and make clean and right what up to now has been dirty and wrong." On and on he went, ending with the idea that it was too bad they were getting married, because that was going to spoil all the fun. The monologue was punctuated with raucous howls of laughter from the audience.

In preparation for this book, I began to watch several of the leading talk shows. One morning a host introduced his special guest, the president of the National Chastity Association, a nationwide organization with branches all over the USA. The moment her title was first announced the studio audience began giggling; when she told what the organization stood for the giggles turned into gales of laughter. One of the panelists was a young man in his early thirties. In a sane and unpreachy manner he shared the destructive results of his earlier sexual promiscuity, his Christian conversion, and his present commitment to celibacy until marriage. During the call-ins from viewers, a twenty-seven-year-old single woman opened her remarks with, "I think this program is absolutely ridiculous." This was greeted by applause from the audience. She then went on to tell with considerable embellishment how much she enjoyed being "sexually active." There was more applause.

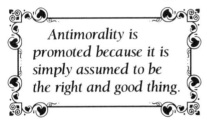

Antimorality is promoted because it is simply assumed to be the right and good thing.

In many ways, our situation is much worse than in ancient Egypt. While it was the *accepted* morality of Joseph's day, it is the *promoted* morality of our day. I am not talking about the immorality or the amorality in today's media. We are far beyond that. I am talking about antimorality—something that appears to be an organized, intentional, and militant movement against Judeo-Christian morality. Let me take it even a step further. Antimorality is promoted because it is simply assumed to be the right and good thing. This is the kind of situation where God Himself cries out, "Woe to those who call evil good and good evil, who put darkness for light and light for darkness, who put bitter for sweet and sweet for bitter" (Isaiah 5:20).

Sexual uncleanness is like a plague that has spread throughout the land, until the married as well as the unmarried are infected. Worse still, this immoral pox has spread to the camp of Christians, even many who call themselves evangelicals. The Scriptures tell us that sex is a good gift of God, to be fully expressed and enjoyed only within a committed, monogamous marriage relationship. In spite of this plain teaching of God's Word, Christians have increasingly bought into the world's philosophy that sex is not a gift but a right to be fully expressed and enjoyed by any two persons so long as they are in a loving, committed, and meaningful relationship. This means that if we Christians want to maintain our God-given vision of sexual purity in both singleness and marriage, we will have to go cross-grain not only to the accepted standards of most of the secular world, but also to the compromised standards of many in the Christian world.

"Use It or Lose It!"

When Potiphar's wife propositioned Joseph, he must have been about twenty-five years old. He was in the very prime of his manhood and sexual desire. If you allow for the differences in age between husbands and wives in those days, Potiphar's wife was probably just slightly older. A woman's sexual desires often intensify during her thirties. There are times and seasons of life, and it would seem in this instance that the strongest temptation came just when both of their natural desires would have been the strongest.

Also notice the unusual description of Joseph—he was "well-built and handsome" (Genesis 39:6). Most of us would be content with just one of those words. To put it in common Egyptian slang, he was a *hunk*! It's no surprise, then, that "after a while his master's wife took notice of Joseph and said, 'Come to bed with me'" (Genesis 39:7). There's an interesting inference that can be drawn. One of the reasons Joseph was tempted was because he was so tempting. He was no cold-blooded mummy, but muscular and masculine, with warm blood running through his veins. Like it or not, some men and women are blessed with physical and emotional equipment that makes them a source of temptation. Joseph had "it," and, as the saying goes, if you have to ask what "it" is, then you don't understand the problem.

By the rest of the story, we know that Joseph wasn't using his attractiveness to tempt her. He was faithfully doing his work and minding his own business. It was Mrs. Potiphar who took the initiative, making use of her feminine charms to seduce Joseph. "[She] began making eyes at Joseph and suggested that he come and sleep with her" (Genesis 39:7, *TLB*). Remember, Egyptian women *invented* eye makeup.

We continually need to remind ourselves that our sexuality is a sacred trust given by God to be used for His purposes. The Creation story tells us that God created us humans "*in His own image ... male and female*" (Genesis 1:27). This means that in some mysterious and marvelous way, both masculinity and femininity reflect the image of God in us. Both are needed to fully understand the nature and character of God, and both have certain God-given characteristics which reveal His true nature to the world. Often we need to ask ourselves, "Am I using my masculinity or femininity to reflect God's character and bring glory to Him?"

In the case of Joseph, where maximum temptation coincided with maximum opportunity, it is a tribute to God's restraining grace that Joseph did not yield. No wonder the Bible tells us four times in Genesis 39, "The Lord was with him." That's for sure!

"I Just Have To Be with Someone!"

Potiphar's responsibilities may have taken him away from home much of the time. Since servants did most of the work, this left his wife alone with time on her hands—a deadly combination, for certainly "an idle mind is the devil's workshop." On the other hand, Joseph was experiencing a different kind of loneliness. In spite of his success and many promotions, he was still a long way from his homeland. He must have missed his father and his kid brother very, very much. So, here were two lonely people: a handsome, lonely man and a beautiful, lonely woman. Never underestimate the intricate connection between loneliness and sexual temptation.

I've heard it innumerable times in my counseling ministry from some of the finest Christian singles I have known, "Doc, I was so lonely. I was okay during the week when I was working, but I just dreaded to see Friday afternoon come because the weekends were so terrible. The most awful kind of loneliness would come over me—it was almost physical, like a blanket or something. It would surround me—I could almost feel it. It got so I just had to be with someone, anyone, and before I realized it I was doing things I never thought I'd do, just to have somebody. I'm ashamed to tell you, it was literally some *body*—just a *body* to touch me and hold me."

We've trained our youth and young adults to cope with all kinds of difficulties—all but one: loneliness. We especially need to prepare future Christian workers to handle this. I have listened to the agonizing confessions of many unmarried missionaries whose lives were moral and clean as long as they were in the protective fellowship of Christians. But in some distant place, waves of loneliness lapping away at their moral shorelines so eroded their souls that the undertow of emptiness and sexual desires pulled them under—and almost drowned their faith.

Let's not forget that sometimes the most painful kind of loneliness is that of the married person who is physically in the same house with a husband or a wife, but emotionally miles apart. Communication has broken down, or the wife has become too engrossed in caring for a child, or the husband is too busy in his work—even God's work—and one partner fails to meet the emotional needs of the other. Soon someone is lonely, although surrounded by people—children, neighbors, and church members. The marriage partner is filling one side of the bed but not the emptiness of the spouse lying so close. That's when the evil one fills even the finest of imaginations with forbidden fantasies and sows the seeds of powerful temptations. What a marvel that Joseph, alone and lonely, was able to resist a love-starved military man's wife.

44

"How Can I Refuse?"

"And though she spoke to Joseph day after day, he refused to go to bed with her or even be with her" (Genesis 39:10). If she had offered herself to him just once, Joseph might have thought, "Maybe I didn't understand what she said," or "She didn't really mean that." But her invitation was repeated, not once or twice, but day after day. She had no doubt what she wanted; she was determined to get it and kept up her seductive suggestions. A man's better judgment might prevail to resist one major attack of sexual temptation. But when it is often repeated, and the woman is so eager and available, even the strongest of men might finally succumb. Well aware of this possibility, Joseph finally decided not to "even be with her."

Paul, advising Timothy, his young "son in the Gospel", tells him there are times when he should fight like a good soldier, discipline himself like a good athlete, and work hard like a good farmer (2 Timothy 2:3-7). However, in the same chapter when it comes to sexual

> *There is a time to stand one's ground and fight, but there is also a time to flee the situation.*

temptations, he says, "Flee the evil desires of youth" (2 Timothy 2:22). There is a time to stand one's ground and fight, but there is also a time to flee the situation. Every good general knows the importance of the "strategic retreat" as one way to ultimately win the battle. If Custer had had the good sense to order his "first retreat," we would probably never have heard of his famous "last stand!"

"From Bedroom to Boardroom?"

Perhaps the most powerful factor in this whole temptation was the possibility of promotion. Remember, Potiphar was Captain of the King's Palace Guard and had an inside track to the Pharaoh. The thought surely must have crossed Joseph's mind that if he agreed to her request, she might possibly agree to a request of his. Just a suggestion from Potiphar's wife could mean a whisper in the ear of Pharaoh by one of his most important officers. Promotion, honor—maybe even freedom—could be the result of an affair with a woman of such high status and influence. By now, Joseph had been there long enough to have heard of such shortcuts to promotion.

The Factors That Held Joseph Steady

When you put all these factors together, from a human standpoint every signal was "Go." How then did Joseph find the strength to say such a positive and permanent "No"?

First, Joseph had a holy dream for his life. The godly vision of his life included the goal of sexual purity. When God gave Joseph his dreams of authority and leadership, He filled him with a sense of self-respect and a commitment to certain moral standards. I firmly believe God used the immoral behavior of several of Joseph's older brothers to turn him the other way and fill him with a determination not to follow their evil example. He knew that if his dreams were ever to be fulfilled, if he were to be lifted above his family, he must never let himself be lowered down to their plane of living.

How does this type of spiritual reaction work in our lives for God's glory? Counselees have shared with me about their own brothers and sisters—sometimes even parents—whose lives were filled with all kinds of immorality. But early in their childhood or youth, God used their very revulsion toward this to fill them with a holy dream—a determination to stay free from such sins and to keep themselves pure for their marriage partners.

Do your dreams include high moral ideals for your courtship and marriage? Don't give up on those dreams. Hold onto them tenaciously. You who are not yet married, keep that vision before you. Don't sell those dreams for a mess of pottage by compromising your standards.

Let me suggest an exercise that has helped others. Write an imaginary letter to your future bride or groom. "But I don't know who that might be," you say. Never mind. Let me reword the suggestion. Write a *real* letter to your *imaginary* bride or groom. Make it a letter which you would like to give to the person on your wedding night, kind of a honeymoon note. Tell this person all about yourself and what you want to give him or her. Then tell what you are expecting on that wonderful night. It's a pretty sobering thought, isn't it? Terribly old-fashioned, awfully square? Yes, and highly Christian too. The reason for my suggestion is that many times I have heard the following from a tearful bride—or groom-to-be. "Oh, if I'd only known that someday I would meet a wonderful guy like _____(or a wonderful girl like _____), I'd never have behaved as I did back in high school or college. I wish I had kept myself clean."

Speaking of letters, let me tell you about a most fascinating one. A dear friend of mine was spiritually mature beyond his years and a gifted preacher. As a young pastor in his late twenties, he was often invited to speak at youth camps, retreats, and revival services in churches. On one such occasion he was conducting a special series of meetings for a church

46

in a distant city. He had been staying in the spacious home of a wealthy
church family. Late one night he was awakened by Jackie, the beautiful
eighteen-year-old daughter of the family. She said she had fallen in love
with him and wanted to have sex with him. Gently but firmly, he talked
her out of it. She returned to her own bedroom embarrassed and in tears.
Seven years later he received a note, the kind one receives from a bride in
appreciation for a wedding present. Puzzled, he checked with his wife who
confirmed that no gift had been sent. They thought it was a mistake until
another tiny note fell out of its folds. It was from Jackie, warmly thanking
him for giving her the most valuable wedding gift she had received—her
virginity!

Our holy dreams can act for God's glory as strongly as Joseph's dream
helped him to remain pure, but there were other factors that also worked
to hold Joseph steady.

Second, Joseph had a strong sense of loyalty and responsibility. At his first
refusal Joseph reminded Potiphar's wife that his master trusted him
completely and had made him responsible for everything. He firmly
believed that to break trust with another human being was a sin: "Everything he owns he has entrusted to my care… How then could I do such a
wicked thing..." (Genesis 39:8-9) Here is a very important moral principle
which we have almost completely forgotten in relationship to sexual
behavior—*our loyalty to and responsibility for the lives of those whom God has
entrusted to our care.*

What is our responsibility? If you are
single and in a dating relationship, your
Master has given you a responsibility for
protecting the sexual purity of the person

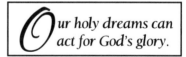

Our holy dreams can
act for God's glory.

you are dating. He or she has been entrusted to your care. This principle
will help answer a question Christian couples ask, "How far should we go?"
Many a young person has assured me, "I am able to control my sex desires,
and I know when to quit." That's only half of the answer! The more
important half is in regard to your partner. Is what you do or want to do
with that person something which will help or hinder them in maintaining control? Each one is responsible for helping the other maintain sexual
purity.

This moral principle is at the very heart of loyalty and faithfulness in
marriage. To commit adultery is to break the commitment and to betray
the trust of the partner God has put into your care. It is also moral "breaking and entering," stealing what does not belong to you by failing to

protect what does. Joseph was held steady by a very high sense of sexual stewardship, and we too are called to the same high standard and responsibility.

Third, Joseph had a tremendous determination not to sin against God. This was the main source of his strength. "How then could I do such a wicked thing and sin against God?"(Genesis 39:9) An ancient legend tells us that when Joseph said those words, Potiphar's wife looked puzzled. Then she smiled understandingly, tore off a part of a richly embroidered drape, and hurrying over to the image of an Egyptian god standing on a pedestal in the corner, threw it over the idol's head, covering its eyes. "Now, Joseph," she said, "it's all right; the god cannot see us." And Joseph is said to have answered, "But my God sees us still. His eyes can never be covered, for darkness and light are both alike to Him."

What a great thought for all of us in our own struggle with lust. Whether it be the hidden caverns of our imaginations when we are alone, or the shadowy corners of an apartment in a secret rendezvous, the words of Psalm 139 apply to us:

> Lord, you have searched me and you know me ....you perceive my thoughts from afar. You discern my going out and my lying down; you are familiar with all my ways ....If I say, "Surely the darkness will hide me ...the darkness will not be dark to you; the night will shine like the day, for darkness is as light to you (vv. 1-3, 11-12).

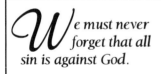
We must never forget that all sin is against God.

Joseph realized that even more than the sin of breaking a trust for which he was responsible, it would be a sin against God Himself. King David realized this *after* he had committed adultery with Bathsheba: "Against you, you only, have I sinned and done what is evil in your sight" (Psalm 51:4). That was the basis of David's repentance. How much better to be like Joseph who realized the sin *beforehand,* for it became the basis of his restraint.

We must never forget that all sin is against God. Cruelty to an animal is a sin against God, by hurting one of His creatures. Polluting the environment is a sin against God, by destroying a part of His creation. And sexual immorality is a sin against God, not only by breaking His law but also by betraying His love.

48

The Price of Purity

Where did all his nobility and purity get Joseph? Truly, as William Congreve wrote centuries ago, "Heav'n has no rage, like love to hatred turn'd, Nor Hell a fury, like a woman scorn'd." So one day, in spite of every attempt to avoid her, Potiphar's wife caught him by surprise and grabbed hold of his coat. When he tried to get away, his coat came off in her hands. When Potiphar returned, she showed him the coat and made up a good story to go with it. Joseph was thrown into prison—the "minimum security" prison where only the king's prisoners were placed, but prison nevertheless (Genesis 39:11-20).

Matthew Henry's commentary on this incident is excellent: "Better to lose a good coat than a good conscience." Yes, this is the second time Joseph has been stripped of his coat; he has kept his character both times. Because he did not yield to sexual temptations, he ended up in prison.

Imprisonment may seem a high price to pay for following one's holy dream, but what would have happened if Joseph had yielded? He would have ended up in a worse prison. The price of his impurity would have been a greater loss of freedom and an even worse kind of imprisonment—in the chains of lust and in the bondage of a secret affair. He would have lost his self-respect and the freedom to continue pursuing his great dream. Jesus said it so well: "I tell you the truth, everyone who sins is a slave to sin" (John 8:34). Nowhere is this more evident than in the enslaving power of sexual sins.

Today, in the name of freedom, many people are losing their freedom. Thinking that the price of purity is too high, they are actually paying an even higher price for their impurity—life in a prison of shattered dreams, regret, and despair.

It is to those of you who find yourselves in that kind of imprisonment that I am now going to address myself—to those of you who think that the Joseph story comes too late to be helpful, since you have already yielded and fallen. God wants to repair the dreams of your past and restore some dreams for your future.

5

REPAIRING BROKEN DREAMS

A few years ago, a well-known speaker came to our community and gave a series of messages to the young people on the theme, "The Christian View of Dating, Sex, and Marriage." I was grateful for his strong commitment to Biblical standards of purity and his helpful suggestions for maintaining them. His conclusions were supported by carefully researched facts and impressive statistics. To my surprise, a large number of students from high school, college, and seminary came to talk to me in the weeks following. Each expressed appreciation for the inspiring talks but then added, "I got depressed as I was listening. It was too late for me; I felt more guilty and hopeless than ever." Then they shared their stories of how they had already messed up their lives sexually. Almost all of them asked the same question, "What do I do now?"

I want to try to answer that question for four categories of people. Although they are all suffering from broken dreams, they face certain distinct problems and need to learn the particular ways of repairing and rebuilding them.

Those Who Became Sexually Involved When Quite Young

In this book I am not thinking about children or youngsters who have been sexually abused and are thus victims of other people's sins. They represent more complicated problems and require special help. I have written rather extensively on this in my book *Healing of Memories*, where I describe ways of counseling and prayer to help restore them to wholeness.

I have in mind preteens, teenagers, high school and college age youth who, through their own wrong choices, have fallen into sexual sins. Research bears out that kids are becoming "sexually active" at an increasingly early age. I personally learned this as a pastor when helping conduct sex education seminars for ten- to twelve-year-olds and their parents. The questions and comments from the fourth- and fifth-graders of today's TV generation are far more frank and clinical than the ones I heard from college students years ago. Some youngsters have had sexual experiences so early in life they have never had the opportunity to create a dream of wholeness. However, I find that for most young people, especially Christians, it is largely during high school and college that their dreams of purity get shattered. Here are some of the most essential ingredients for mending these tattered dreams.

   Receive God's full and free forgiveness. Does it seem too simple? I do not mean it to sound that way because it really isn't. In fact, there's something different about sexual sins which seems to make forgiveness more difficult to receive. They make us so ashamed and guilty that we feel we can't come to God, can't even enter His presence, let alone ask Him to forgive us. Here are just a few of the many ways I've heard these sentiments expressed. "I feel so dirty—I can't talk to God in this shape." Or, "I knew better. It was my own fault. My best friend warned me, God Himself even warned me, but I didn't listen. How can I come and ask Him to help me now?" Or, "But Doc, you don't understand. This happened *after* I was saved. How can God forgive me for doing that, after He has done so much for me?" And, "I've been such a fake. I've been Miss Goody Two Shoes," or "They call me 'Mr. Clean' in the youth group at church. If they knew what a hypocrite I really am! I feel too phony to talk to God."

> *The great accuser of our souls regularly tries to tell us we are not good enough to come and ask God for His free gift of forgiveness.*

There are many different places these feelings might be coming from. One thing is sure—they are *not* coming from God. They may sound like conscience or the voice of God, but they aren't. One of your old childhood tapes could be playing back the familiar voice of a critical, unpleasable parent, a legalistic Sunday School teacher, or a graceless and judgmental preacher. Or your own severe perfectionism could very well be laying the lash on yourself. And using these or other possible sources of condemnation is our ancient enemy—Satan himself. He doesn't want to see us succeed; and so the great accuser of our souls regularly tries to tell us we are not good enough, not clean enough, not sincere enough, and not repentant enough to come and ask God for His free gift of forgiveness. Of the many great Scriptures which assure us of God's everlasting mercy and forgiving grace, there is one

52

passage which I have always found especially effective in dealing with
youth struggling to find forgiveness from the guilt of sexual sins
(Psalm 25:4-7, italics and caps mine).

> Show me your ways, O LORD,
> teach me your paths;
> guide me in your truth and teach me,
> for you are God my Savior,
> and my hope is in you all day long.
> Remember, O LORD your great mercy and love,
> for they are from of old.

> *Remember not the sins of my youth*
> *and my rebellious ways;*
> *according to your love remember me,*
> *for you are good, O LORD.*

1. Seek help from others. Sometimes we cannot seem to reclaim the
assurance of God's forgiveness by ourselves. It is then that we need to enlist
the help of a trusted friend, a youth minister, pastor, or counselor in our
battle. I'm not sure why it is especially true of sexual sins, but I have found
that they, almost more than any others, need the special strategy of agreed
and united prayer. In Matt. 18:18-20, Jesus Himself reminds us of the
high-voltage power of such prayer to "loosen" those who are bound.
James 5:16 instructs us, "Therefore, confess your sins to each other and
pray for each other so that you may be healed." I often follow such a time
of prayer with Holy Communion. Many have testified that it was while
partaking of the bread and the cup that they gained the victory in this
particular battle, finally feeling forgiven and clean once again.

One reason that sharing and praying with others is such an effective
strategy is that it breaks false pride, restoring true self-respect. The low
self-esteem and the self-flagellation which accompany sexual sins are not
necessarily signs of true repentance and humility; they may be the result of
our falling below the high estimate we had of ourselves. We are angry
because we didn't think we could ever do such things. Others could, of
course, but not us. That super self (superior self) picture we had of
ourselves got all smashed up by our real self and gave a terrible blow to our
pride. There is no better cure for such pride than sharing the truth about

ourselves with others and having them pray for us.

There is another reason for letting others in on our problem. It provides not only *support* but also *accountability*. I increasingly find that the only way some Christians can maintain their purity is by becoming part of a group of people committed to helping one another achieve this goal. Sometimes the power of lust can be so strong that only an accountability group can break its hold over us. This is especially true when pornography, exhibitionism, compulsive masturbation, promiscuity, or other forms of addictive sexual behavior are involved. Many church communities today have discovered the importance of confidential and redemptive small groups for Christians caught in this kind of prison.

2. Let God give you a new kind of holy dream. Don't allow the apparent loss of certain options to push you into forever accepting lower standards. Satan wants to fill you with such despair and pessimism over losing your original dream that you will say, "What's the use? I've already fallen from my highest standards, so I might as well throw them all away."

These were almost the very words Virginia, a young college student, used to describe her feelings to me. It was a story I've heard hundreds of times. The characters and places may be different but the plot is pretty much the same....A good home, moral and churchgoing, sometimes deeply Christian; at other times, at least nominally so....Parents with high standards, a mother who was open and helpful, talking freely with her daughter about the facts of life and the importance of keeping herself pure for marriage. A no-nonsense father who let Mother talk about "such matters" but who strongly, almost angrily, upheld high standards—he'd "take care" of any guy who messed with his daughter. Virginia's story fit this pattern. She appreciated her parents and emphasized that what had happened was not their fault but hers.

Virginia had dated a lot, gone steady a couple of times in high school, but had never violated the moral standards she had set for herself. She was waiting for Mr. Right Guy, who—so it appeared— came along in college. Tim had everything she had dreamed about: good looks, brains, athletic ability, and best of all, he claimed to be a Christian. They went steady for over a year and a half. There was a strong physical attraction between them. "It got to be pretty high voltage," Virginia said, "and we kept going further and further with our making out. I kept crossing limits I had set for myself. I prayed a lot about it, but I could never bring myself to talk with Tim about it. As much as I tried, whenever we crossed a line I could never seem to uncross it. Finally we went all the way. I was ashamed and I vowed, "Never again," but we did. I told myself it was okay because we would get married someday. Then the strangest thing happened. Tim seemed to lose interest in me and began to find excuses to cool our relationship. Within weeks we had broken up, and he was looking at someone else. I was absolutely devastated and got terribly depressed. I wanted so much to talk to Mom, but I was afraid she'd tell Dad, and I didn't know what might happen. While I was feeling so down, this other guy invited me out. He was a real pro, and by the second date we had gone all the way. The next time this happened, I knew I had to do something about it; that's why I'm here."

Virginia began sobbing. "My Mom used to remind me of what my name meant. Big deal! Look at me, Virginia, only I'm just 'i-a' now, I've lost the 'Virgin' part. Ever since I went all the way, something inside me keeps saying, 'You blew it, kid, you've lost it. You might as well go ahead; it doesn't make any difference now.'"

Virginia and I spent several hours talking and praying together. In our last session, after we had shared in Holy Communion, I laid my hands on her head and prayed for her. During my prayer I said something like this: "O Lord, since You have given Virginia the gift of complete forgiveness for her sins, and washed her clean in Your love, I ask that You will now give her an even more wonderful gift. Restore to her a full sense of her purity. Let her feel completely pure and clean once more. Lord, never again let her call unclean what You have called clean."

She later told me that my prayer completely shocked her, for she had never thought of anything like that. But later it dawned on her that though there was no way to restore her virginity, God had restored her purity, and within a few days had restored her self-esteem. Years later, she told me that this restored her vision of keeping pure until marriage and enabled her to accomplish that goal.

That is exactly what God can do for you. In fact, He wants to do more than that. He wants to take what was once your weakest point and turn it into your strongest. No longer are you naive or innocent or ignorant. You are no longer foolishly unaware of your capacity for sin. Now you are wisely aware of it, and this can drive you to a much deeper dependence on God for your strength. You know exactly what you might do, given the right temptation and the wrong circumstances. So you not only pray, but you watch *and* pray, lest you even enter into temptation. With the past fully forgiven, your holy dreams restored, and your present lived in total

God wants to take what was once your weakest point and turn it into your strongest.

reliance on the Holy Spirit's power, you can then live in victorious confidence of the future. You can say with Paul, "For when I am weak, then I am strong" (2 Corinthians 12:10*b*).

Courting Couples Who Are Having Sex Together

Here are my special words of advice to you.

Countless Christian couples feel they must get married because they've already had intercourse. Rather than face the truth about the relationship, they feel they must marry out of a sense of guilt. They reason this way: "Although we have done wrong, it will be all right if we go ahead and get married." Don't let your feelings of guilt push you into an unhappy marriage.

Some people assume incorrectly that marriage retroactively absolves us of anything we may have done prior to it. I find this notion especially in women. They are usually more spiritually sensitive than men and can make peace with the situation only by constantly telling themselves, "It's all right—after all we *are* going to get married." This common rationalization has no basis in the Bible.

It's far better to repent now than to regret later. Better to face your guilt and spend hours confessing it together, than to ignore it and spend years in conflict and unhappiness. Don't misunderstand me. I am *not* saying that because you have already become sexually involved, you should necessarily punish yourselves by not getting married. That might be equally destructive, since you two may be the right ones for each other. Please consider the following advice:

1. Test the reality of your love for one another by sexual abstinence and by seeking counsel. Unless you back off physically, it is almost impossible to determine whether what you feel is genuine love or merely sexual attraction. This will not be easy to do and it's unlikely you will be able to do it by yourselves. Seek out a counselor or spiritual mentor to whom you make yourselves periodically accountable. Also, let this person help you understand and communicate about your differences. Such a person can be invaluable in helping you discover whether or not you have the true Christian love and respect necessary for a good marriage—a love which can stand the test of time, distance, and mutually-agreed physical restraint. This period of testing will clarify your motives and desire, enabling you to make a *free* decision about your future—together or apart. For those who do this and decide upon marriage I have the following suggestion.

2. Rebuild your dreams and your self-respect. Along with your present commitment, set a wedding date in the reasonably near future. Be realistic about your own weaknesses and strengths in this area, even though you are in a covenant of accountability. At this point I often become very direct and advise couples to move up their wedding date. Sometimes they tell me their parents will not understand, but when I urge them to share the problem with their parents these couples are usually pleasantly surprised by the sympathetic response they receive. If they are not, then with the couple's permission, I talk directly to the parents on their behalf. In my experience, the father of the bride is usually the greater problem. So I talk with him "man to man," and in frank but guarded ways explain the situation. In every case, the parents have been anxious to cooperate.

I stress this because a wedding date provides a definite timeline and goal toward which everyone can work. This provides the motivation needed to keep the couple's commitment to sexual abstinence. Thus they continue their personal disciplines and corporate accountability right up to the time of their marriage. I have helped scores of couples do this and afterward have always heard this kind of comment, "It was really tough, but we sure are glad we did it. For when we walked down the aisle and stood at that altar we didn't feel like a couple of guilty phonies. We literally held our heads high, because with God's help we had rebuilt our own self-respect and our respect for one another!"

Those words speak to the heart of the matter. To rebuild self-respect is to regain one's self-esteem. When we do this, we succeed in repairing our broken past and are well on the way to restoring our high and holy dreams for marriage.

Married Couples with Broken Dreams

When people are feeling desperate, they often think only of their own pain. At times like these, their urgency to get help overrides all normal thinking; and, because they forget time zone differences, the ringing of the telephone has frequently awakened me out of a deep sleep!

One such night the caller was Beth, the wife of a former student. They had been in the ministry for several years. Beth was all apologies when she realized what time of night it was for me. But when I heard her story, I was glad she had called. She and her husband Stan had been outstanding students and our children in the Gospel. He was a born leader, a gifted preacher, and had already built up a large congregation who loved him very much. I was shocked when Beth told me with tears in her voice that Stan was going to quit the ministry. "He's already made up his mind. He's written a letter of resignation and plans to give it to the elders this week and announce it from the pulpit next Sunday." She then explained that unknown to her, Stan had had a long-standing problem with pornography; recently, quite by accident, a member of the church had seen him buying some pornographic magazines in a distant city. Stan was ashamed and afraid, and his own sensitive conscience troubled him greatly. He had just opened his heart to Beth and told her of his lifelong battle with sexual fantasies. Also, he told her that of late he had begun to mentally yield to them and allow for the possibility of some "inappropriate behavior" with women in the church. He was grateful that God had restrained him, but he was feeling very guilty, utterly unworthy to be a minister. He thought the only solution was to confess this to his congregation and resign as their pastor.

I then talked to Stan, and over the next few days we had several long conversations. I told him I thought the devil was trying to push him into punishing himself and destroying his ministry, and under no circumstances should he follow through on his plans. I advised him to call his elders, confess everything to them privately, and seek their forgiveness. Then, if the elders wanted him to stay, he should request them to hold him accountable in the future.

Reluctantly and fearfully he did this. Much to his own surprise and joy, the elders were completely sympathetic. They very much wanted him to continue as their minister and agreed to meet with him regularly. They were not in the least interested in punishing or humiliating him, but in saving him for the ministry. He is still at that church and God has given him an even greater and more effective ministry—beginning with some of the elders who, touched by his honesty, began to deal with their own deep needs. Beth certainly struggled with personal disillusionment and some shattered dreams; but through forgiveness, open communication, and further counsel, her dreams for both their marriage and their ministry have successfully been rebuilt.

Some Christian couples face much more extensive problems; their sins have moved past fantasy and into action. Nothing produces more broken dreams than extramarital sexual involvement. There is always a terrible sense of betrayal on the part of the wounded spouse. Let me share some important suggestions based on many years of helping such couples.

Deep wounds tend to reopen and take a long time to heal.

Mutual trust is like a bridge; when broken it takes a lot of time to repair. Many couples think because they are Christians, they are exempt from this principle. They expect their spouses to be able immediately to put their weight down on the bridge. This is a mistake. Broken trust cannot be restored quickly. Guilty spouses, even though they have truly repented and confessed to their partners, must not be surprised when they occasionally experience outbursts of hurt and anger from their spouses. Deep wounds tend to reopen and take a long time to heal. This is one of the prices to be paid for infidelity. Lasting healing requires a lot of prayer and patience on the part of *both* partners. Many men try to hasten this process by trying to restore sexual relationships too quickly. Don't rush the physical side of marriage. Work at rebuilding trust and restoring emotional and spiritual relationships. The sexual aspect will follow as a serendipity.

Don't underestimate the addictive power of a sexual involvement, and the struggle the unfaithful spouse will have with the pull to return to the affair. Again and again I am asked, "But can't we just be friends? Do we have to become enemies? Can't I just be with him/her once in a while?" There must be a positive decision to break off *all* contact with the person and make no allowance for the possibility of a recurring sexual involvement. This is a prime example of our battle in enemy territory. While innocent partners need to understand the struggles their spouses may undergo with the terrific pull of the emotional and sexual bonding which grips them, they must also be uncompromising about insisting on a clean break in order to succeed.

Let me say a word to counselors who are working to help such struggling persons. When someone tells me in a counseling session that he or she feels powerless to change his or her feelings, I always agree: "Of course you can't change those feelings. That's not your responsibility. God can, and your part is to tell God you are willing for Him to change your feelings. Are you willing to join with me in prayer and offer Him your willingness?" This is another area in which regular participation in Holy Communion helps to break the power of canceled sin and set the prisoner free.

Somewhere in the healing process, there comes a time when both parties need to make a covenant with God and each other that the "affair" will never again be brought up by either one, and never be used as a means to excuse wrong behavior, elicit self-pity, or get back at each other in any way. This is the last span to be riveted onto the rebuilt bridge of trust. Trust can now be complete—trust that the spouse will never mention it again in any connection.

Deep disillusionment and despair accompany the broken trust and shattered dreams of unfaithfulness in marriage. However, there is another side to the story. Such situations, when faced with courage, repentance, and confession, can bring both the divine and human forgiveness which results in miraculous healing. Like mended broken bones, those marriages, by God's healing grace, can be stronger than ever. The marital dreams can be restored, shining brighter than ever.

Divorce or Widowed Persons Living Alone

In our last chapter we dealt with the close relationship between loneliness and sex and the strong temptation to fill emotional emptiness through sexual involvement. This problem is greatly heightened for divorced and widowed people. Most of them have known, at least for a time, the joys and ecstasies of married love. It's hard for them to be satisfied with lesser expressions. This need, added to the terrible gnawing pain of being alone, can produce a powerful inner compulsion toward sex. Because many of them feel great fear of commitment to another lasting relationship, they are strongly tempted to temporary sexual liaisons.

Having been on the inside of several church ministries to the divorced, I have dealt with scores of such persons who have fallen into this trap. Several young women, fighting to keep themselves pure, have told me that there are some men who look at the church as a "kind of Christian singles bar where you can find partners for casual sex." Many who work in singles ministries have confirmed that this is not an exaggeration; they constantly have to be on guard against this in their groups. Let me make a few suggestions for the divorced and widowed people who want to maintain their dreams of holy sexuality.

Brooding keeps us bound to the past, and robs us of the spiritual energy and clear thinking we desperately need to cope with the present.

Keep your heart free from bitterness and resentment. God's Word warns against the "root of bitterness" which can arise in our hearts and result in defiling many (Hebrews 12:15). Why do I put this first? Because angry and hateful thoughts toward a former mate can fill us with wrong motives for establishing new relationship; this, in turn, gives the devil a foothold for sexual temptations. Here are a few bitter motives which have been shared with me: "I'll show him there's someone who thinks I'm still attractive." "I won't let his early death be the end of my sex life." "I'll prove to her that there is a woman who wants me." "I'm going to prove to him/her that I'm not as bad as he/she said I was." "How could God take my husband/wife? I need to be close to someone." "I'll show him—he thought I couldn't get along without him!" "She made me feel totally unwanted, but look at all the women who want me." In almost every case, this kind of bitterness fueled the fires of sex and led to an affair, or even promiscuous sex.

Furthermore, brooding over the hurts and injustices of a broken marriage or the pain of loss keeps us bound to the past, and robs us of the spiritual energy and clear thinking we desperately need to cope with the present. We literally are "so mad we can't think straight," and will end up in irrational and self-destructive behavior. A later chapter in this book, "Forgiving the Dream Destroyers," will help you find grace to forgive and keep your heart clear of hate and bitterness.

Concentrate on holding steady for the first year, for it is going to be the hardest. How often I've heard these sentiments expressed, "The first few months were hell. I wasn't sure I was going to make it. But after a year or so, I learned how to cope." These people were describing primarily the pains of loneliness and shattered self-esteem, but they often included their battles with strong sexual temptations. Again and again such people had a way of just hanging around after the church services were over. Then when most people had gone, they would say to Helen or me, "Just give me a hug. You don't know what it means to me. I've been having such a rough time." A young divorcee gave me a word picture I have never forgotten, "I felt like there was a hole in my heart as big as the Grand Canyon, and I was tempted to fill it in any way I could."

There is a great opportunity for the church today to provide the right kind of supportive fellowship for such hurting and tempted people. Sunday School classes, couples with strong and healthy marriages, senior citizens, and others need to be urged and organized to give emotional, spiritual, and often financial help in holding divorced or widowed persons steady, especially during the first year or two. In addition, the church must provide the special grace, counsel, and wisdom for those who re-marry, making sure theirs is a truly Christian decision. Many churches not only fail to do what we have been describing but, through judgmental and condemning attitudes, actually drive many divorced persons out of their protective fellowship and into sinful relationships. This is a tragedy and travesty on the true redemptive nature of Christ's Body in the world.

Let God, by His grace, reshape your dreams. No one has a higher view of marriage than Helen and I do. We have given ourselves unreservedly to maintain this high ideal. In the past years, we have led over 1,000 couples through Marriage Enrichment weekends, and an even greater number of engaged couples through Engaged Discovery weekends. But in a fallen world, and a "wicked and adulterous generation" (Matthew 12:39) which is literally falling apart, we have found our ministry must also provide grace to those whose original dreams for marriage have been shattered. When all possible doors for reconciliation have been closed, we have also spent many hours in helping divorced Christians carefully and prayerfully make right choices for the future. This is the time when they need to abandon their former dreams and leave all the guilt connected with their brokenness at the foot of the Cross. By so doing, they will no longer cling to unrealistic dreams and unrealizable options. Because these are gone forever, they must be relinquished into the hands of the One who specializes in turning second chances into something very special. One of the most important factors in this process is helping people maintain their vision of sexual purity, for this provides a strong foundation for building new dreams. We have watched God wonderfully use many such couples as wounded healers to other hurting people.

Uphold a standard of purity. In his commentaries, William Barclay claims it was the Early Church's uncompromising stand on sexual purity, in contrast with the moral rottenness of the times, which attracted people from all over the world who were looking for something better. I believe the same thing happens to our decaying society, when the Church once again upholds Biblical standards and challenges people to pay the price of sexual purity.

At the same time, we must also proclaim the Biblical doctrine of restorative grace to those who fall below those standards. This is what Paul did when writing to such persons in the immoral seaport town of Corinth. After referring to the worst possible sexual offenses, he said, "And that is what some of you were. But you were washed, you were sanctified, you were justified in the name of the Lord Jesus Christ and the Spirit of God." Finally, he reminded them that their bodies were "a temple of the Holy Spirit, who is in you, whom you have received from God" (1 Corinthians 6:11,19).

6

DREAMS IN THE DUNGEON

Some time later, the cupbearer and the baker of the king of Egypt offended their master, the king of Egypt. Pharaoh was angry with his two officials, the chief cupbearer and the chief baker, and put them in custody in the house of the captain of the guard, in the same prison where Joseph was confined. The captain of the guard assigned them to Joseph, and he attended them.

After they had been in custody for some time, each of the two men—the cupbearer and the baker of the king of Egypt, who were being held in prison—had a dream the same night, and each dream had a meaning of its own. When Joseph came to them the next morning, he saw that they were dejected. So he asked Pharaoh's officials who were in custody with him in his master's house, "Why are your faces so sad today?"

"We both had dreams," they answered, "but there is no one to interpret them." Then Joseph said to them, "Do not interpretations belong to God? Tell me your dreams."

So the chief cupbearer told Joseph his dream. He said to him, "In my dream I saw a vine in front of me, and on the vine were three branches. As soon as it budded, it blossomed, and its clusters ripened into grapes. Pharaoh's cup was in my hand, and I took the grapes, squeezed them into Pharaoh's cup and put the cup in his hand."

"This is what it means," Joseph said to him. "The three branches are three days. Within three days Pharaoh will lift up your head and restore you to your position, and you will put Pharaoh's cup in his hand, just as you used to do when you were his cupbearer. But when all goes well with you, remember me and show me kindness; mention me to Pharaoh and get me out of this prison. For I was forcibly carried off from the land of the Hebrews, and even here I have done nothing to deserve being put in a dungeon." (Genesis 40:1-15)

It is impossible to know the thoughts that raced through Joseph's mind on that fateful day when, because he rejected Potiphar's wife, he was accused, arrested, and thrown into prison. He did what was right. He refused to betray his master's trust or break his commitment to God. Why did it turn out all wrong? Just when he could see the possibility of his dreams being fulfilled, they were once again thrown into a pit. As that prison door clanged shut, he must have wondered about the God who had kept him from sinning but not from suffering. We know the depth of Joseph's despair, for in Genesis 40:15 we hear the pathos as he says to the cupbearer, "I have done nothing to deserve being put in a dungeon."

Did you realize there is another account of this in a later Scripture? Retelling the history of Israel, the psalmist tells us:

> When He summoned a famine on the land,
> and broke every staff of bread,
> He had sent a man ahead of them,
> Joseph, who was sold as a slave.
> His feet were hurt with fetters,
> his neck was put in a collar of iron;
> until what He had said came to pass
> the word of the Lord tested him.
> The king sent and released him,
> the ruler of the peoples set him free;
> he made him lord of his house,
> and ruler of all his possessions,
> to instruct his princes at his pleasure,
> and to teach his elders wisdom.
> (Psalm 105:16-22, *RSV*)

Tested—God is going to test Joseph and his dreams in that dungeon. It is the worst kind of testing, for it's one thing to be tested or tried when you are guilty, but quite another when you are innocent—when your very purity has apparently caused the injustice. That's the hardest kind of testing to endure.

Let us consider some of the testings which come to us. As we look at them through the perspective of Joseph's prison years, we can hear God's relevant message for us. Paul, in speaking of other ancient incidents in the life of God's people, assures us it is appropriate to do this. "Now these things which happened to our ancestors are illustrations of the way in

64

which God works, and they were
written down to be a warning to us who
are living in the final days of the present
order" (1 Corinthians 10:11, *PH*).

> *The hardest kind
> of testing to endure is when
> your very purity has appar-
> ently caused the injustice.*

The Dungeons of Darkness

The Bible speaks of many types of darkness which are the result of sin.
However, it is wrong to conclude that all times of darkness come directly
from our own sin. Certainly Joseph's darkness didn't, and there are many
times when our darkness doesn't either.

*There are other kinds of darkness which God can and does use to disci-
pline His children.* Job speaks of these when he says, "He has blocked my
way so I cannot pass; He has shrouded my paths in darkness" (Job 19:8).
Jeremiah shares the same sentiment, "I am the man who has seen affliction
... He has driven me away and made me walk in darkness rather than
light" (Lamentations 3:1-2).

Sometimes there is what we might call the darkness of dryness. This is the
darkness which some of the saints have described as the seeming with-
drawal of any feelings of God's presence from the soul. Instead, there is a
strong sense of His absence. Such a time of deep spiritual aridness is called
by various names: "the long dark night of the soul," "a spiritual desert,"
"the wilderness of the soul." It is God's discipline of darkness so that we
will stop walking by *sight* and learn to walk by *faith* (2 Corinthians 5:7).
After all, our moments of great spiritual feeling and ecstatic joy really do
not require much faith, for the delights and gifts of God buoy us along by
themselves. So in order for us to grow and to grow up, God allows the arid
times to teach us to depend only on Him, so that *we will love not just the
gifts but the Giver—God Himself.* We will learn to love God for who He is
and not just for what He gives.

A. W. Tozer said:

> Feeling is the play of emotions over the will, a kind of musical
> accompaniment to the business of living. And while it is indeed
> enjoyable to have the band play as we march to Zion, it is by no
> means indispensable. We can work and walk without music, and
> if we have true faith we can walk with God even without feelings.[1]

The discipline of dryness teaches what no other course in God's curriculum can teach quite so effectively: that spiritual feelings can come and go
without altering our true relationship with Him. This is a commonplace

realization for everyone who has walked with God for any length of time. But we live in a "spiritually sensate" generation. The spirit that demands heroes in every crisis, literary masterpieces in every magazine, and TV spectaculars every week has infected us Christians. "Have you had your miracle for today?" Time in the darkness of dryness tempers and strengthens our faith to believe without any supporting delights.

Then there is the darkness of dilemma. I am referring to those dark moments of life when we honestly try but seem unable to discover what God's will for us really is. We are in darkness regarding God's direction for us, or regarding some decision we are forced to make. In these times, we don't seem to get any flashes of light or answers to "fleeces" (see Judges 6), or openings of doors.

Many years ago, at a critical juncture in our lives when we were faced with a difficult decision, someone sent my wife and me a small card with three quotes printed on it:

> *Confronted by an inescapable choice*
> *and not knowing what to decide,*
> *I have found that <u>unhurried waiting upon God</u>*
> *never fails to clarify the issues*
> *and to lead me to know exactly what to do.*
> Archbishop William Temple
>
>
>
> *I have never lacked guidance—<u>only obedience</u>.*
> Rufus Mosley
>
>
>
> *If any man <u>will to do His will</u>, he shall know ...*
> John 7:17, KJV

I was never able to verify the first two quotes. The words of Jesus are in a slightly different context—that of "knowing" the truth about His teachings. The underlined words, however, were relevant to our dilemma. The more I studied the card, the clearer the message became. Jesus did not say, "If anyone will *do* His will"—for one may not know what that will is. Rather, He said that if anyone just *wills* to do His will, or as the NIV translates it, "chooses to do God's will ...." All He asks is that we set the direction of our will in the direction of doing His will, and ultimately God will make the way plain. I saw my mind and will as a blackboard upon which God wanted to write His instructions. But He could do that only if I first made sure my mind was erased clean of my own will so that I could clearly read the direction He would write.

A famous architect—when telling about his work of designing houses—said that when clients came asking him to draw up plans, he soon discovered most of them had already designed their homes. What they wanted was for him to sanction their plans, and then draw blueprints for what they had already decided. He wished that they would come without a lot of preconceived notions, so that he could help them discover what would be best for them.

As I listened, I thought how much we are like these people, and how often God has to discipline us with dark times. When the dilemma is so great that we

> *All He asks is that we set the direction of our will in the direction of doing His will.*

are forced to abandon all our own plans, we will wait for Him to write His design on the clean slate of our minds.

A recently licensed pilot was flying his private plane on a cloudy day. He was not very experienced in instrument landing. When the control tower was to bring him in for a landing, he started thinking of the hills and towers and buildings in that area and began to get panicky. In a calm but stern voice the command came, "You just obey *in*structions; we'll take care of the *ob*structions."

Yes, if anyone sets his mind in the direction of obedience to God's will, He will handle the obstructions. He will take care of the darkness and turn it into light.

Keeping the Darkness Out of the Heart

Joseph was in a dungeon of darkness that could easily have turned into a dungeon of despair and depression. This reminds me of someone describing a woman who had passed through some bitter experiences. They said it was as if the darkness had crept into her heart and darkened her eyes. At this point we realize one of the most remarkable secrets of Joseph's life—the darkness which surrounded him in that cell was not allowed to enter his heart. The light of the dream within him was kept burning bright and clear. There was no space for the darkness to enter and darken his spirit.

In his book *Born Again*, Charles Colson tells of his involvement in the

Watergate scandal, his subsequent Christian conversion, and then his seven-month imprisonment. He describes what a struggle it was to keep a truly Christian spirit during his confinement. He watched some of the strongest men finally give in and turn into ambulatory vegetables while in prison. Some slept every minute they could, as a way of escape. Some turned in on themselves, and their very bodies followed their minds, brooding and drooping until they were bent over and shuffling around the prison. They degenerated both physically and mentally. Colson says he avoided that only by the strongest determination—by strict physical disciplines like walking fast, exercising regularly, and fighting off sleep except at night, and by keeping his mind on God through regular Bible study and prayer. Only by a strict ordering of himself was he able to keep the prison from getting inside him.

> *Joseph was inside the dungeon—but he never let the dungeon get inside him.*

Let's not miss the simple but important lesson which God wants to teach us through all this. Life never consists of just three dimensions: time, space, and events. There is always a fourth—our response to the three dimensions. The key issue is not *what* happens, and *where* and *when*, but *how* we respond to what happens. That's where the word *responsibility* comes from: our ability to respond. A little poem I learned in school says it so succinctly:

> Two men looked out from prison bars.
> One saw mud, the other stars.

Joseph was inside the dungeon—but he never let the dungeon get inside him. Imagine what his thoughts about his brothers could have been. They were the real culprits who started this chain of events. How easily he could have become a prisoner to self-pity and seething resentment. He could have dwelt on the incredible injustice which had resulted from the lies and false accusations of Potiphar's wife. If he had done that, the darkness of the dungeon would have gotten inside of him and, slowly but surely, would have turned into the darkness of despair and depression. The truth is that one of the major causes of depression is repressed, slow-burning anger. Instead of giving in to angry feelings, Joseph kept his heart pure and his conscience clean. Although he was in prison, he never allowed himself to become a prisoner of cynicism and bitterness. Once again, "The Lord was with him," keeping his spirit free by keeping his heart pure.

During Joseph's prison experience, we see the same thing happening to him that had happened back in Potiphar's house. Joseph proved to be a person of integrity amidst the sordid treachery and cruelty of prison life. Before long he was made chief assistant to the warden and was actually running the day-to-day business of the prison. Remember Joseph's dream? Once again the sheaves were bowing down before his sheaf and he was in a position of authority and leadership.

One day the king's cupbearer and baker were thrown into the same prison. Since they were important persons on Pharaoh's palace staff, they were put into Joseph's custody. One night both men had disturbing dreams. The words of the story are remarkable. "When Joseph came to them the next morning, he saw that they were dejected, so he asked Pharaoh's officials ... 'Why are your faces so sad today?'" (Genesis 40:6-7) In spite of all his own troubles and unjust sufferings, Joseph had not lost his compassion. Suffering often turns us in on ourselves, so engrossing us in our own pain that we fail to be sensitive to the hurts of others. Only if we keep self-pity and bitterness out of our hearts will our suffering make us tenderhearted and responsive to the suffering of others. The moment Joseph saw the two men, he sensed something was wrong and immediately offered himself as a listener.

In *Born Again*, Colson tells that when he first entered prison, an old-timer advised him, "Mind your own business, and whatever you do, don't get involved." Colson comments that the man was detached from reality and almost schizoid. Colson became all the more determined to get involved, to listen and love, and try to help others.

With a compassionate spirit, Joseph listened to the men's disturbing dreams. Then, giving full credit to God, he interpreted their dreams for them. Exactly as he had foretold, within three days they were both released—the baker to be hanged and the cupbearer to be reinstated to his former high position. In this incident, we see not only Joseph's compassion but his humanity. We can almost hear the quiver in his voice when he makes that special request of the cupbearer: "When all goes well with you, remember me and show me kindness; mention me to Pharaoh and get me out of this prison. For ... I have done nothing to deserve being put in a dungeon." What a wistful plea. "I'm innocent, I really don't belong here any more than you did. Please, when you get out of here, put in a good word to the king for me."

And what happened? Was the cupbearer so filled with gratitude that he went out of his way to beg for a special pardon on Joseph's behalf?

Absolutely not. And here is the *third* time Joseph is thrown into a pit—this time by a thoughtless and ungrateful official.

The Dungeon of Disappointment

So Joseph stays on in the prison. At first his spirits are high with hope. But as the days lengthen into months, he begins to realize the terrible truth! "The chief cupbearer, however, did not remember Joseph; he forgot him" (Genesis 40:23). Now the darkness of that dungeon is "blacker than a thousand midnights down in the cypress swamp."[2]

The great British essayist Frank W. Boreham tells of the first explorers in Australia who were led by Hamilton Hume. While leading a band of pathfinders from Sydney to Melbourne, they experienced a great crisis. They came face to face with a range of mountains now known as the Hume Range. Utterly worn out, the party begged to be allowed to give up and return home. Hume pointed to a high mountain just ahead and said, "No, we must climb that. From that summit I'm sure we'll see the ocean and can go back and tell the others of our success." So after a desperate struggle they climbed the mountain. But when they reached the top, one can imagine their utter despair when all they could see was miles and miles of ridges and gullies, all covered with trees. The goal they had dreamed about was not even in sight. It is to their everlasting credit that they kept on going and finally did arrive. (They named the mountain *Mount Disappointment*!)

We've all experienced it. We've all known the awful feeling in the pit of our stomachs which disappointment brings. Let me take you back to the story of my family's personal Dothan (see Genesis 37:17-28), which I began in chapter 3—the death of our son. The weeks which followed were dark and empty. Then slowly we began to see how God was using even that traumatic event. In spite of the fact that I had been born in India, lived as a child in that very town, and could speak the local language without an accent, there were still walls between us and the people. Now, through the loss of a child, we had become one of them, for almost every Indian family around us had lost at least one of their children. We were no longer some special heavenly messengers, exempt from the sorrows of life. Old walls began to break down and new doors open up. When a year later Stephen, our second son, was born, our Indian friends joined in our excitement and celebration.

It was during this time that God literally poured out His Holy Spirit upon us. A great revival, which began in the central church at Bidar, spread throughout the entire area. Lay persons, filled with newfound joy and zeal, fanned out over the villages, witnessing to unreached relatives and neighbors. Because of the caste system with its unique sociological structure, people in rural India rarely make individual decisions. Instead, they make decisions as entire households or castes, even the decision to accept Christ's salvation! In this way everyone in the village belonging to a particular group, after a period of careful instruction and examination, receives baptism and a new congregation is formed. Thus, the Spirit began a new "mass movement" in our area, so that for several years we were baptizing over 3,000 new Christians annually.

At the same time, we saw what some called "a glorious epidemic"—rural congregations building churches for themselves. The backyard and garage of our house became a miniature factory, turning out trusses, windows, and doors for these buildings. For several years an average of one church a month was constructed! Although the money for permanent roofing and skilled labor was given by friends in the USA, the land, the building materials, and all unskilled labor was provided at great sacrifice by the people themselves. By 1954, the central school had become a large high school, the hospital was overflowing with patients, and a whole new church district had been created because of the continuing growth of the church.

We had been enjoying considerable publicity throughout our denomination back home. One day I told Helen of my enlarged and extended dream and excitedly said, "You know what? I want to stay here for at least twenty-five years and build at least 100 churches!" Helen shared the joy of the dream. She too was happy in the work, and as a wife and mother she was especially pleased with the lovely new home our mission had built for us. It was on a slight elevation, had a beautiful view, and was away from the unhealthy atmosphere of our former bungalow.

We were so thrilled by it all that we did not see the gathering clouds. The rapid growth of the church in our area had not gone unnoticed by less friendly eyes. It was written up in some state newspapers and discussed in the Parliament at New Delhi. A political factor played a large part in what was going to happen.

Our home was in Bidar, part of Hyderabad State, the largest and most powerful of all the princely "native states" which made up British India. Though its population of twenty million was mostly Hindu, its Nizam (maharajah) was a fanatical Shi'ite Muslim whose dynasty had ruled the area for centuries. Back in 1947, when India had become an independent country, Hyderabad was the *only* state which declared its own independence and refused to join the Indian Union. After trying to settle the issue through peaceful negotiations, India finally sent in its army and forced the state to become a part of the new nation.

During that brief but very real five-day war in September of 1948, through the unbelievable providences of God, another missionary and I had actually surrendered our town to the Indian army. It was utterly ludicrous—two American missionaries and an Indian army colonel riding in the lead vehicle, a twenty-year-old Chevrolet ambulance painted with the sign *Methodist Mission, Sunshine Dispensary*, followed by World War II—vintage light Sherman tanks, gun carriers, and a train of trucks carrying heavily armed troops! It was ludicrous but important, for the key military town of Bidar was taken peacefully and a great many lives were spared. We were officially thanked for this by the Commanding General of the Army.

However, there were others in the local Hindu populace who had never forgiven us for this, even though several years had passed. To their way of thinking, we had prevented them from taking revenge on the town's Muslims for the centuries of tyrannical oppression which the Hindus had suffered.

In early 1955, some highly-placed Christians cooperated with militant Hindus and other enemies of the church to cause the storm which finally broke over our heads. I was falsely accused of "kidnapping and forcibly detaining" someone. This led to my arrest and release on bail. My moral character was attacked and false witnesses backed up the accusations. Perhaps the most traumatic incident took place early one morning when I discovered a dead newborn lying outside our back door. The police discovered it had actually been dug from its shallow grave and put there. The final blow came when one of the Hindu men, who had been the angriest about our part in the 1948 military incident, became the head of the government department which handled permits for missionaries. We were grateful to be allowed to stay in India, but the order came for us to leave our beloved Bidar. Thousands of Christians who loved and appreciated us gave us an unforgettable farewell and wept with us on that desperately dark day.

Since there was no other similar mission station to which we could go, I ended up in downtown Bombay. For the next ten months I sat behind a desk and served as assistant treasurer in our main office. The great loves of my life—touring in my Jeep, preaching, evangelizing, baptizing, planting congregations, and building churches—had been cruelly wrenched from me, leaving a terrible hole in my heart. I would stand out on the balcony of our seventh floor apartment and cry out, "God, why have You forsaken me?" It was truly our dungeon of disappointment, for our dreams had been destroyed.

Is there anything worse than our disappointment in others? Especially when their actions have caused your plans and dreams to be broken? What can God's purpose be in allowing such things to happen? It is to teach us full dependence on Himself through the discipline of detachment from others. He brings us under this discipline in many ways.

An example of this can be seen in the disappointments we experience in courtship and romance. Many young people I have counseled seem to believe that every new romance is life's

> *Often He allows us to spend time in a dungeon of disappointment to disentangle us from idolatrous attachments.*

great curtain going up, and every broken one is life's great curtain coming down—forever. This also applies to relationships within marriage. Husbands or wives can become much too dependent on their partners for happiness and fulfillment. Parents can fall into the trap of a ravenous and possessive attachment to their children. Our problem is that some of us go beyond merely wanting someone; we are in grave danger of worshipping the person—allowing a human being to fill the throne in the heart that is for God alone. Often He allows us to spend time in a dungeon of disappointment to disentangle us from idolatrous attachments to persons or plans, possessions or places.

Corrie ten Boom has said, "I have learned not to hold on to things too tightly, for it only hurts more when God pries my fingers away from it." As I look back on the time spent in our dark dungeon of disappointment, I am now able to thank God for His steadfast love. His *agapé* love always desires the best for the one loved. I realize now that if things had gone on as they were, I would probably have spiritually self-destructed. I was drowning in my own successful statistics and didn't know it. Above all, I was caught up in the busy, busy, busyness of it all. God needed to fill in many of the hollow places in my soul. He needed to heal my damaged emotions, and at the time I wouldn't have known a damaged emotion if I had run into one in the middle of the street. I wasn't even aware of a whole layer of my own emotional and spiritual needs, let alone equipped to help others with theirs.

Also, Helen and I needed to work on so many things in our marriage. We were an MK and a PK whom God needed to make OK so we could minister to hundreds of hurting couples in the years to come. This would never have happened without God allowing our original dream to be tested and tried and found wanting so He could replace it with a brand-new one. The author of Hebrews speaks of the way God gave us "the greater" and "the better" in Christ, and states the divine principle we learn through our disappointments: "He sets aside the first to establish the second" (Hebrews 10:9*b*). We found the well-known lines of a simple poem to be true for us:

> Disappointment ... His appointment,
> Change one letter, then I see
> That the thwarting of my purpose
> Is God's better choice for me.
> His appointment must bring blessing
> Though it may come in disguise,
> For the end from the beginning
> Open to His wisdom lies.

The Dungeon of Delays

Returning to Joseph's story, a year passes and Joseph is still in prison. Then another year has gone by, and he is thirty years old. It is now thirteen years since that seventeen-year-old dreamer started out across the fields to visit his brothers. Where are his dreams now? And where is the God who gave him those dreams?

O we of little faith. We are still asking the same question, aren't we? God is going to give us the answer pretty soon, but first He wants to teach us about the dungeon of delay.

God uses the dungeon of delay because He has to get us onto His divine timetable. Many times He cannot do this without taking us through the discipline of delay and detour. In experiences of unchosen and enforced waiting, God wants us to wait upon Him. In the hurry and pressure of life, including life in God's service, *activity* has replaced *receptivity*, and few of us spend adequate time waiting on the Lord.

Someone has said that Christians have passed through three phases in the last half century. First, we had the "Holier Than Thou" period with its overemphasis on legalism and personal holiness tending toward Pharisaism. Then we went to the opposite extreme of "Guiltier Than

Thou," and in the name of exalting justification by faith alone, we became careless of personal ethics. Now we are in the worst stage of all—"Busier Than Thou," in which we measure our Christianity by our activities, results, and statistics. How sad!

This is why God often allows situations in which we are forced to wait upon Him. Illness is one of those situations. When we are flat on our backs, we are forced to

> *God uses the dungeon of delay because He has to get us onto His divine timetable.*

look up to God. Again and again I've heard it said following serious surgery or a long period of recuperation, "I wouldn't have chosen it for anything, and I sure wouldn't want to go through it again, but I really thank God for all the wonderful things He has taught me during this time."

Another one of life's great interrupters is an unplanned pregnancy. Many a distraught wife has come for help and said through bitter tears, "I don't understand *how* this could have happened. We were doing everything we could to prevent it. But mainly I can't understand *why* God allowed it. It's the worst thing that could have happened to us at this time! Our other children are just getting to the age where I could be free to ..." and then she shares her plans for finishing a long-awaited degree, or getting a job which would finally enable them to live without financial worries, or joining with her husband in more direct Christian service. Don't underestimate the emotional and spiritual struggle that this unchosen dungeon of delay can bring to even the finest women. However, this is where we see a great divide between the pro-abortion and pro-life people. The pro-abortion advocates don't understand God's promise of "sufficient grace." With Christians, while there are many unplanned pregnancies, there are few unwanted children. Years later, those very same wives joyfully share their pride and joy in these very same children, and then go on to tell the wonderful way God used those years to bring them to a new depth of intimacy with Himself.

Interrupted dreams are not necessarily broken dreams meant to be abandoned. They are only delayed dreams—meant to be postponed. Remember, God-given dreams will keep in the deep-freeze of acceptance, provided you keep out any heat from resentments. Then, at a later time, you can thaw them in the microwave of freshly warmed hope and determination. This is often the way God's discipline of delay and detour works out in our lives.

Joseph's dreams for a speedy release never materialized, but God continued to keep him faithful in what the saints of old described as "doing the duty that lies nearest." They meant that while we have to wait, we are to be good and faithful servants in the task we have been given to do. The thankless cupbearer continued to forget him; but Joseph continued, without bitterness or cynicism, to be a faithful assistant to the warden of the prison.

> *Interrupted dreams are not necessarily broken dreams meant to be abandoned.*

Finally, "when two full years had passed, Pharaoh had a dream" (Genesis 41:1). In fact, he dreamed twice in that same night, once of seven fat cows which ate up seven lean cows, and once of seven healthy heads of grain which swallowed up seven scorched heads of grain. He dreamed so vividly that he couldn't shake the images out of his mind the next morning. Pharoah called in all his magicians and wise men, but they could not figure out the meaning of those weird dreams.

Can you imagine the atmosphere in the palace—everybody treading around on tiptoe, afraid of Pharoah's wrath? Naturally the cupbearer learned about the troubling dreams. After all, the king had lost his appetite. Then the cupbearer shook his head in shame, and confessed, "Today I am reminded of my shortcomings" (Genesis 41:9). He told Pharaoh all about his and the baker's dreams while they were in prison, how a young Hebrew in the jail with them had interpreted those dreams, and how everything had come out exactly as he had predicted (Genesis 41:10-13).

Now we understand the reason for the delay. If the cupbearer had told Pharaoh about Joseph when he had first gotten out of prison, Pharaoh would have probably said, "Uh-huh" and gone on with his meal. But now, *two full years later*, Pharaoh immediately responded because he desperately needed someone like Joseph. The next verse is a real thriller: Pharaoh sent for Joseph and "he was quickly brought from the dungeon" (Genesis 41:14). The discipline of delay was over, the detour ended. Joseph was *now* on "God's speedy schedule"! So what did he do? Did he rush right into the presence of the king and tell him everything he knew? No, he had learned a lot by his enforced disciplines—perhaps most important of all, how to discipline himself. "When he had shaved and changed his clothes, he came before Pharaoh" (Genesis 41:14). What

76

greater proof that Joseph's spirit had not been broken by years in that dirty prison, surrounded by evil strangers, and forgotten by ungrateful friends! Because he had maintained his high self-respect and self-esteem, he wanted his body and his clothes to be as clean as his soul. He knew that to talk to a king he needed to be prepared, and to represent God before Pharaoh, he needed to be a fit representative.

Life has a way of being consistent, so that the inner and the outer often match each other. Joseph had been faithful in the little things and now God was going to make him a ruler of the big things. God had taken Joseph to Potiphar's house, but in order to fulfill his dreams, God had to get him into Pharaoh's palace. That result had required the delay and the detour of the palace prison.

My wife and I experienced this also. Following our time in Bombay, we were still uncertain about our missionary service. We went for a short time to another rural mission station where it was thought I would return to my evangelistic work. Unfortunately, it was during the monsoon season, and that year brought record-breaking rains—the worst we had ever seen. My four-wheel-drive Jeep could hardly get out of the driveway, let alone navigate the impassable village roads. The countryside was a veritable sea of mud. One day as I sat looking out the office window watching it rain, I felt as if I were in a dungeon of darkness, distress, despair, disappointment, and delay all wrapped into one humid, wet blanket. Deep in my soul, I began another one of my arguments with God. Didn't He realize what all this was doing to me? "Me—David Seamands, unable to do anything. All my many talents being wasted in this overgrown, muddy village."

Then as clear as crystal the inner voice of the Spirit said to me, "David, keep the division of labor straight. If it's My will that you spend the rest of your life in this overgrown, muddy village, then that's My business, not yours. Your part in all this is to dig down and go as deep as you can. That's your business. You take care of the depth, and I'll take care of the length and the breadth." I cannot explain it, but something inside me clicked back into place for the first time since that gloomy day in Bidar. It was God's way of restoring and refashioning my dream.

It rained for the next two months, producing serious floods in an otherwise dry area. During that time, in addition to studying the Bible, I read fifty books. I digested them, filing their contents, and God gave me a lot of wonderful ideas. I would need these ideas in the days to come. It wasn't long before we were sent to a large inner-city pastorate in

Bangalore where we spent six years. Then we came back to the States to Wilmore, Kentucky, and Asbury College and Seminary. We did not know that God was going to change the entire course of our lives as well as the contents of our dream. But now we understand it was all an important part of His discipline of delay and detour.

7

INTERPRETERS
FOR GOD

*T*hen the chief cupbearer said to Pharaoh, "Today I am reminded of my
shortcomings. Pharaoh was once angry with his servants, and he
imprisoned me and the chief baker in the house of the captain of the guard.
Each of us had a dream the same night, and each dream had a meaning of
its own. Now a young Hebrew was there with us, a servant of the captain
of the guard. We told him our dreams, and he interpreted them for us,
giving each man the interpretation of his dream. And things turned out
exactly as he interpreted them to us: I was restored to my position, and the
other man was hanged."

*So Pharaoh sent for Joseph, and he was quickly brought from the
dungeon. When he had shaved and changed his clothes, he came before
Pharaoh. Pharaoh said to Joseph, "I had a dream, and no one can interpret it. But I have heard it said of you that when you hear a dream you can
interpret it."*

*"I cannot do it," Joseph replied to Pharaoh, "but God will give Pharaoh
the answer he desires" (Genesis 41:9-16)*

At long last Joseph was a free man. But the sheer exhilaration of that
moment was tempered by the dangerous fact that he now stood before the
highest authority of the land—the mighty Pharaoh himself—who pos-
sessed the power of life and death. Only a truly mature, God-filled person
could possibly handle the intoxication and the ambivalence of such a
moment. Never do we see such qualities more evident in Joseph than after
Pharaoh's flattering words, "I had a dream, and no one can interpret it.
But I have heard it said of you that when you hear a dream you can
interpret it." Joseph replied, "I cannot do it, but God will give Pharaoh
the answer he desires" (Genesis 41:15-16). Joseph's humble response must
have made a good impression on Pharaoh, for at once he began to tell

Joseph all the details of both dreams.

As the famous King of Siam used to say, "It's a puzzlement." The most curious part is not the dreams themselves, but the fact that the magicians and wise men of Egypt were unable to interpret them, since the dreams were so thoroughly Egyptian. No country was as river-centered as Egypt. It has been accurately called "the gift of the Nile." Even today Egypt is totally dependent on the river for its existence. Out of the Nile really do come either the good years or the bad years, the fat cows or the lean cows, the full ears of harvest or the blighted ears of drought. In those days, long before such colossal water-control projects as the huge Aswan Dam, the Egyptians were completely dependent upon the river's annual rise and overflow for the irrigating of their crops and the watering of their cattle—the very basics of life itself.

An ancient Egyptian legend illustrates their pride in the Nile's life-sustaining capacities. Once upon a time the gods decided to call all the rivers of the world before them in order to determine which was the greatest of them all. Each river was to represent its own case and tell why it should be considered the greatest. The Tigris-Euphrates said that it had been the cradle of both creation and civilization. The Ganges of India retorted that it was by far the most sacred—people made long pilgrimages to wash away their sins in its waters. One by one each made its claim, until only the Nile was left. It seemed hesitant, for it had nothing upon which to base any distinction. Finally, urged on by the gods, it said, "The only thing I do is that twice a year I overflow my banks." According to the legend, when the gods heard this, they agreed that it was the greatest because it brought *life* to the most people.

The Egyptians worshiped the river. They also reverenced the cow as the symbol of the reproductive power of nature. If God wanted to show Pharaoh that seven years of plenty were coming, he couldn't have said it in plainer language than the Egyptian dream-symbolism of seven fat cows coming up out of the river to feed on the lush green of its banks. Pharaoh himself, who had no doubt often gone down to the river to sacrifice, might possibly have understood the dreams without the aid of his wise men. I believe that what troubled Pharaoh so much, and what kept the soothsayers from interpreting the dream, was the shuddering premonition which followed: seven lean, starving, bone-protruding cows came up out of the Nile, "scrawny and very ugly and lean. I had never seen such ugly cows in all the land of Egypt" (Genesis 41:19). And the dream grew more frightening, for even after they had eaten the fat, sleek cows, "no one could tell

that had done so; they looked just as ugly as before" (Genesis 41:20-21).
The second dream was similar: "The thin heads of grain swallowed up the
seven good heads" (Genesis 41:24*a*).

I believe the magicians understood the obvious meaning all too clearly
but were afraid to tell Pharaoh. After all, in those days you could lose your
life for making a king unhappy. The Old Testament is filled with false
prophets who were afraid to tell kings the truth, and a few true ones who
were imprisoned when they did!

Qualifications of God's Interpreter

As Joseph became an interpreter for God, he was so filled with the Spirit
of God that he was endowed with wisdom and discernment. Therefore, he
was completely sure about the message of the dreams. This certainty gave
him the courage to tell the King both the "good news and the bad news"
contained in the dreams. Most important of all, it gave him the confidence
to propose God's plan of deliverance from the terrible prediction of the
dreams.

Joseph told Pharaoh that God was saying the same thing in both dreams
so that he would be sure to get the message that God was ready to make
these dreams into reality in the very near future. There were shortly to be
seven good years, with monsoon rains and an overflowing river, resulting in
bumper crops for the entire country. These would be followed by seven
bad years of drought, destroyed crops, famine, and starvation. Before
Pharaoh could press the panic button or call for his execution, Joseph
proceeded to outline God's plan of salvation from the impending disaster
(Genesis 41:25-36). Pharaoh was to appoint commissioners over various
areas of the country who would collect twenty percent of the harvest
during the seven bountiful years and store it in special government grana-
ries. This food would then be rationed out and sold to the people during
the seven years of famine. In this way the nation would be preserved. And
to carry out this plan, Pharaoh was to "look for a discerning and wise man
and put him in charge of the land of Egypt" (Genesis 41:33).

"The plan seemed good to Pharaoh and to all his officials"
(Genesis 41:37). After all, it was so simple a child could understand it,
and yet so profound in its possibilities that Pharaoh intuitively recognized
the presence of God in Joseph:

"Can we find anyone like this man, one in whom is the spirit of God?"
Then Pharaoh said to Joseph, "Since God has made all this known to
you, there is no one so discerning and wise as you. You shall be in

charge of my palace, and all my people are to submit to your orders. Only with respect to the throne will I be greater than you…I hereby put you in charge of the whole land of Egypt" (Genesis 41:37-41).

Joseph went from the darkness of the dungeon to the dazzling brightness of the throne in a single bound.

There is not another "prison to palace" story in all of history to compare with this one. Joseph had suggested finding a secretary of agriculture, but Pharaoh had appointed *him* the Prime Minister of the nation! Joseph went from the darkness of the dungeon to the dazzling brightness of the throne in a single bound. His father had rebuked him for that dream about the sun and the moons bowing before him, but here was Pharaoh—the greatest monarch of the day—welcoming him. His brothers had despised him, but now the proudest priesthood in the world would receive him into its ranks by marriage to a favorite daughter. His hands, callused from the toils of a slave, would now wear Pharaoh's own signet ring. His feet, once bound by iron chains, would now rest firmly in Pharaoh's second chariot, and a chain of gold would lie around his neck. Yes, for the third time Joseph has lost his coat, but this time it is to be replaced by the fine linen robe of state.[1]

It all happened because Joseph had faithfully clung to the high and holy dream that God had given him years before.

- What if Joseph had become bitter or resentful or cynical when his brothers sold him into slavery?
- Or if he had yielded to the daily seductions and temptations of Potiphar's wife and done what everybody was doing in those days?
- Or if he had taken any of the shortcuts available to the scheming and the unscrupulous of the times?
- Or if he had rotted in that prison, wallowing in self-pity and hate because someone had thoughtlessly forgotten his helpful services?

Had he done any of these things, do you think he would have been filling this high position, appointed by a pagan king because even he recognized him to be God's man for the hour? Joseph succeeded in enemy territory because at every step of the way he had faithfully lived out his own dreams and faithfully interpreted the dreams of others.

Interpreters for God Today

God was able to use Joseph so effectively because he had a sensitive spirit to the needs of others. While in prison he had noticed the sad and dejected faces of fellow-prisoners, and this had led to the opportunity of his becoming an interpreter of dreams and a witness for his God. In the same way, God wants us to be His interpreters today. Our spiritual radar must be sensitive to the faces and the feelings of others as they tell us their needs. As in Joseph's case, our interpretation of God's message must speak to people where they are. It must be addressed to their particular situation and their felt needs.

We need to get in the habit of looking at people's faces, listening to their words, and trying to understand their unspoken messages. When we do, we, like Joseph, will see people with sad and dejected faces. We will notice lines that come from worry and hear the tones of voice that indicate they are carrying heavy loads. Keep in mind that when we do this, we—like Joseph—will be faced with unanswered questions, unexplained sufferings, unsolved problems, unattained dreams, uninterpreted myster-ies, and even frightening confrontations with life and death. It was the great New England preacher Joseph Parker who said that those who minister to troubled hearts will never lack for a congregation. Since many in that congregation will have little knowledge of God's Word and less contact with the church, *we* must learn to become interpreters of the crises of their lives. In this way, we will help them navigate the shoals of life in such a way that they gain character and faith in God's ultimate "good plan."

Let us think of the events surrounding some of the most common experiences of life which represent dreams that need interpreting.

The birth of a child. New life can be an occasion of great joy and celebration, or disappoint-ment and disturbance, sometimes even tragedy and grief, when abnormalities or defects are involved. Even in the most ideal situation it means reorganizing the home, redesigning everyone's routine, and always that painful process of redistributing love. If you are a sensitive Christian, the whole experience can be a great opportunity to help people interpret their dreams.

> *We need to get in the habit of looking at people's faces, listening to their words, and trying to understand their unspoken messages.*

I have always wondered at the story behind these words of Scripture: "When Enoch had lived sixty-five years, he became the father of Methuselah. And *after he became the father of Methuselah, Enoch walked with God 300 years*" (Genesis 5:21, 22, italics mine). Up to that point Enoch was just another ordinary man in that long list. What was it about the birth of a son that changed him so greatly that he began his close walk with God? We don't know for sure, but I've seen transformation in the lives of a seemingly unconcerned couple upon the birth of their child. Often it is the overwhelming sense of responsibility which forces them to acknowledge that they need help beyond themselves to fulfill their dreams for the child. It's often a wide-open opportunity for us to help people interpret what it means to share with God the miracle of creation.

The death of a child, including miscarriage and still-birth. Someone needs to bring not only comfort but understanding to such tragedy. This is borne out by the many individuals who struggle with resentment against God, and also by the surprising number of married couples who—instead of comforting and supporting one another—end up divorcing as a result of their child's death. Interpreting for God doesn't necessarily mean having all the answers, quoting the most Scripture verses, or bombarding parents with simplistic statements about "God's will."

During the loss of our son, Helen and I found that such Christians were the least helpful of all. Interpreting may mean acknowledging the presence of mystery by just being there—by loving and listening without thinking it necessary to give explanations. The gift of a good book, written by someone who has gone through the same grief, can be wonderfully helpful. From our empathy and tears, bereaved parents can learn that God too cares and hurts with them as they grieve over the loss of a dream.

The waywardness of a child. Sometimes in spite of stable homes and good parenting, children can still get into serious trouble. A son gets involved in drugs, or a teenage daughter becomes pregnant, and parents are filled with a hundred and one questions and an equal number of guilty self-incriminations. Shattered dreams fill their thoughts during the day and crowd out sleep at night. The victorious Christian walk can seem like an impossible dream to those suffering through such heartache.

Many of Jesus' examples involved the parallels between human and divine parenthood. During difficult situations, people may see for the first time God's suffering love and painful concern for His wayward children (Luke 15:11-32).

Marriage and divorce. All around us we hear the sounds of marital dreams being broken. To me it is like the shattering of a beautiful piece of wedding crystal that has been dashed to the floor. On the faces of divorced people, we see the lines of loss, loneliness, desperation, and financial anxiety. Many times they say, "It would have been much easier if she/he had died." In divorce, unlike death, you keep seeing the corpse.

84

Divorce is perhaps the most devastating blow to a person's self-esteem. Unfortunately, divorced people all too often get a critical and condemning attitude from Christians and the church. If we would only follow the example of our Lord who always loved and accepted people, even when He did not approve of their behavior! Then we would translate God's amazing grace for the undeserving and the broken into the understandable language of everyday relationships. Our own marriages, families, and churches would become like cities of refuge for the divorced, where they could become a part of the family of God. In a few instances, old marriages might be reconciled and the broken dreams restored. Often, though, we need to help these hurting people to reconstruct new dreams for their lives, built on the one sure foundation, and upheld by the fellowship and support of Christ's people.

Suffering and death. As I mention this, you may be feeling overwhelmed and thinking, "But I'm not a pastor or counselor. I'm a layperson. I want to be sensitive to these kinds of opportunities to witness for God, but I'm not sure I know *how*. I need instruction and help." An excellent book, which covers the gamut of such subjects, is *Helping People through Grief* by Delores Kuenning, published by Bethany House. It is a sensitive guide created to help you know how and when to share your concern with people in crisis and pain. Such books can enable you to become one of God's interpreters for today.

In the preface of her book, Delores Kuenning reminds us that "earth has been called a vale of tears," and then gives statistics which verify that fact. Each year in the United States...

- Two million people die
- On the average, one person dies every five minutes due to accidental injury
- 462,000 die annually from cancer
- 120,000 die from Alzheimer's disease
- One out of every twenty-one babies dies during the first year of life
- Approximately two million people suffer from burns; of these, 70,000 will be hospitalized and 12,000 will die
- There are annually two million stroke victims
- 125,000 victims of spinal cord injury
- 140,000 brain-injured persons who enter rehabilitation programs

Yes, in the midst of life, we are literally surrounded by suffering and death. As Christians who do not grieve as those without hope (1 Thessalonians 4:13), we have the only true words of comfort to give people. But we cannot do this out of a vacuum; we must speak from a prior loving, caring relationship with the person. We cannot make up for the lack of such a relationship by all of a sudden becoming compulsively concerned about a person's salvation. People rightly resent this and do not hear our Christian interpretation of death. Let us make sure we establish relationships that we can build on in crisis times. John Greenleaf Whittier's poem says it well:

> *The dear Lord's best interpreters*
> *Are humble human souls.*
> *The Gospel of a life*
> *Is more than books or scrolls.*

Translating Wants into Needs

Many people do not wear sad and dejected faces. On the surface, they seem to be successful and happy, without any sense of felt need. They have a great many wants and desires and think that if those are filled, they will be satisfied. How do we become God's interpreters to such people? We have the difficult but challenging task of helping them understand that even if those many wants are satisfied, their true needs still remain unmet. We are interpreters in the sense of translating their temporal wants into spiritual needs. Isaiah clearly understood this as he cried out:

> Come, all you who are thirsty, come to the waters;
> And you who have no money, come, buy and eat!
> Come, buy wine and milk without money and without cost.
> Why spend money on what is not bread,
> and your labor on what does not satisfy?
> Listen, listen to Me, and eat what is good,
> And your soul will delight in the richest of fare.
> Give ear and come to Me;
> Hear Me, that your soul may live (Isaiah 55:1-3*a*).

A few years ago, we had an older student in the seminary who had given up his rank as a senior officer in the Naval Air Force to enter the ministry. One day I heard him tell how this came about. He said that from his early youth he had had a dream about being in the Navy and was determined to reach the top of the ladder. He had worked hard and his dream had come true. His next promotion would be to Admiral. But one day God, working through the changed lives of transformed people, had drawn back the veil and shown him the shocking truth. As he so aptly puts it, "Although I had indeed reached the top of the ladder, I suddenly realized the ladder was leaning against the wrong building!" His dreams had turned out to be false and empty mirages. Although his wants had been fulfilled, his deepest needs could be met only when Christ entered his life.

Let's make sure we are on the lookout for those whose outward status and success hide deep inward emptiness. To be an interpreter for God means asking the Holy Spirit for the wisdom to take people where they are, to express what they think they want, and to interpret those wants so that they will come to discover what they really need.

In the story of Joseph, Pharaoh was troubled and afraid. He thought he needed a magician to supply a right interpretation of his dream. What he really needed was a way out, a plan of rescue. He needed what Joseph was able to provide for him—a deliverer and savior.

One night in 1960, a handsome young Hindu knocked at the door of our home in Bangalore, India. He introduced himself as a student at the university working on a Ph.D. in electronics. He was interested in American

> *"Although I had indeed reached the top of the ladder, I suddenly realized the ladder was leaning against the wrong building!"*

jazz and said he had heard that we had a stereo and a good collection of records—like the classics of Glen Miller and others. What he had heard was true. That kind of highly-arranged jazz has always been a hobby of mine. I invited him in, and within minutes we were listening to the music of the big band era and eating some of Helen's delicious fridge-made ice cream—a specialty of hers. This began a close friendship with the youth who turned out to be from a wealthy, high-caste Hindu family. He had come to the city from a distant state. He was a long way from his parents and felt lonely and homesick.

His visits continued for more than a year without any mention of religion. Then one unforgettable night, as we were listening to a record by the "King of Swing," Benny Goodman, he suddenly got up and said, "Could we talk in your office?" As soon as we were alone he asked me, "Brother David, what does it mean to be a Christian?" I shared with him very briefly, then loaned him a book by C. S. Lewis and a tape by E. Stanley Jones. In our times of discussion together, I discovered that he was concerned not to deny the good things his parents had taught him, the noble and high ethical principles he had received from their religious teachings. Again and again I had to assure him that to receive Jesus Christ was not to deny any of the ethical teachings he had received, but to find in Him their fullness. Finally, during one memorable night, he surrendered himself to Christ, the One who is the way, the truth, and the life, and the fulfillment of humankind's religious aspirations. A few months later, on a beautiful Easter Sunday morning, along with a Buddhist family, a Muslim youth, and a young Jewish lady, he received Christian baptism. He paid a heavy price for his decision because his orthodox Hindu family immediately disinherited him, but to this day he is a dedicated Christian. Helen and I look back with joy on what we called our "jazz and ice-cream evangelism days" when, as interpreters for God, we had to translate what people *wanted* into what they really *needed*.

> *People's images of God are formed when they are children and are largely based on their experiences with their parents or caregivers.*

Children Need God's Interpreters

Perhaps the greatest single group of persons needing interpreters for God are our children. James Fowler, the director of the Center for Faith Development at Emory University, is a world-renowned expert on children and the Christian faith. In hundreds of individual interviews he has found that people's images of God are formed when they are children and are largely based on their experiences with their parents or caregivers. For example, he found that children whose parents were arbitrary or abusive were likely to think of God as one who can punish without warning and who looks at us as having little worth. These children think of themselves as bad and deserving of bad treatment. When parents are predictable, positive, and loving, their children tend to think of God as caring and of themselves as valuable.

Most of us do not need a word from the experts on this. We are all living proof of it, either as a curse from which we need to be delivered, or a blessing for which we are grateful.

I have already written about my own earthly father and how he made it much easier for me to believe in my loving Heavenly Father. However, one thing Dad was not was a good preacher. My brother J. T. and I agree that Dad was one of the worst preachers and the best "live-ers" we ever knew. Probably one of the best examples of this is a "sermon" he preached when I was just seven. On a beautiful morning prior to Christmas 1929, when we were living in Kolar, India, a letter arrived from the Mellon Bank of Pittsburgh with the crushing news that my folks' entire life savings had been lost when the bank failed. My mother wept bitter tears as she sobbed almost hysterically. I didn't understand it all, but I knew by the somber look on Dad's face that it was something pretty serious. Then we all knelt in prayer, and Dad talked with God in his own inimitable way. He reaffirmed complete trust in our Heavenly Father to take full care of us and meet all our needs out of His riches in Christ Jesus. Though I didn't know it at the time, I now realize that this was one of the great sermons of my life—an enacted parable in living color and stereophonic sound. Since I fully trusted my father, and he fully trusted his Father, that meant that I too could fully trust the Father.

Contrast this with a pastoral experience I once had. A fine Christian man in his mid-forties came to counsel. He was a PK (preacher's kid) and spoke appreciatively of his Christian upbringing. But in spite of all of his sincere spiritual disciplines, he never seemed to be able to develop the kind of close, intimate relationship with God he had always longed for. God seemed distant and almost uncaring. After some time of talking together, I asked him to tell me the picture of God that came to his mind when he tried to relate to Him. He thought for a while and then described this scene. God was seated at a desk, his swivel chair turned around so that His back was turned. He sat facing vast bookcases of encyclopedias and reference books containing all the knowledge and wisdom He needed to run the universe. The man explained this was what he *imagined* God was like in the office, since he had never even gotten inside; there was a sign on the door which said, "Please Do Not Disturb." God was so busy keeping the Milky Way and the planets in order that He couldn't be concerned with our petty problems. Even as my friend told me this, he apologized for it. "I know it's ridiculous," he said. "I know God isn't really like that, but it's the way I feel about Him—and the way I think He feels about me."

After a few sessions together we were finally able to discover where this picture had come from. It was a scene that had taken place on many a Saturday when he was a youngster. He wanted his father to come out and play with him, but he was always busy in his office. And there really had been a sign like that on the study door. After several rebuffs he had stopped even trying and had just gone out and played by himself. Why *couldn't* his dad come out to spend time with him? He was too busy preparing sermons so that the next morning he could get up in the pulpit and tell people how much God loved them!

Interpreting the Scriptures

Nowadays we are surrounded not only by millions of Biblical illiterates, but also by a vast number of people whose misunderstandings of Scripture give them a gross misrepresentation of God. Their caricatured concepts of God keep them out of the Kingdom. Others who are Christians are prevented from spiritual maturity by their wrong use of the Bible. Hebrews describes God's Word as "living and active, sharper than any double-edged sword" (Hebrews 4:12). A single-edged sword used carelessly is dangerous enough. It can cut and wound someone else. But a double-edged sword is even more dangerous, for it can wound us as well as others.

The need for someone to interpret God's Word is as old as Scripture itself. Philip was led of the Spirit to join the chariot of the Ethiopian treasurer, and found him reading from Isaiah 53. Philip asked him, "Do you understand what you are reading?" To which the official replied, "How can I, unless someone explains it to me?" The *New English Bible* translates it, "How can I understand unless someone will give me the clue?" We are then told that as they traveled together Philip "began with that very passage of Scripture and told him the good news about Jesus." His timely interpretation led to the baptism of this high official a few miles down the road (Acts 8:26-38).

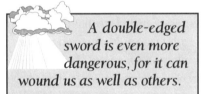
A double-edged sword is even more dangerous, for it can wound us as well as others.

As we travel down our particular road of life, let us become alert to the large number of people who need to be given the greatest clue: Jesus. He is the clue to a proper understanding of Scripture, for He is the full and final revelation God has given us of Himself. In a sense, the Bible is the only book we should read backward. We begin with Jesus, the *last Word* God gave us on who and what He is really like, and then read backward to the *prior words*, interpreting them all in His light. The Bible everywhere recognizes this gradual and progressive unfolding of God's revelation. This was not because God was changing, but because He could reveal Himself to people only as they were able to receive more and more of the truth.

> In the past God spoke to our forefathers through the prophets at many times and various ways, but in these last days He has spoken to us by His Son, whom He appointed heir of all things, and through whom He made the universe. The Son is the radiance of God's glory and the exact representation of His being (Hebrews 1:1-3*a*).

Jesus Himself told His disciples, "If you really knew Me, you would know My Father as well. From now on, you do know him and have seen him" (John 14:7).

It is so important that we help people to read and interpret all Scripture, as Paul puts it, in "the light of the knowledge of the glory of God in the face of Christ" (2 Corinthians 4:6*b*). There are certainly many things, particularly in the Old Testament, which are difficult to understand. We must see this period as a time in which God slowly but surely shone a brighter and brighter light upon His face until He revealed Himself in the face of the one who is the Light. This means we must commit ourselves to serious Bible study, not just memorizing proof texts from here and there in Scripture, throwing them together in a kind of Biblical tossed salad, and serving it up to people with our own particular house dressing. We need to understand the full-orbed message of Scripture and, like Philip, interpret every passage in the light of the good news of Jesus.

The best interpretation of all is a person whose life translates the grace and truth of God into everyday living. It was the great physicist Robert J. Oppenheimer, in a speech regarding the spread of democratic ideals, who said, "The best way to export an idea is to wrap it in a person." Joseph was God's message wrapped in a person.

Will you too be an interpreter for God? A modern Joseph who watches people's faces, listens to their questions, and with God's help interprets their dreams and their nightmares? In humility but authority, in tenderness as well as courage, will you live out the good news and the bad news before them—the bad news of our lostness and famine outside Christ, and the good news of our foundness and fullness in Him?

No wonder Pharaoh gave Joseph a new name, *Zaphenath-Paneah*, "bread of life!"

8

FORGIVING THE DREAM DESTROYERS

I had just finished speaking at a morning service on "Emotional and Spiritual Wholeness" and was now at the retreat center cafeteria looking around for a place to sit. A woman at one of the round tables caught my eye; since she was alone I felt hesitant to join her. But the impression that I should sit by her grew within me until finally I walked over and put my tray down beside her. The moment I did this she said, "Thank God. I was praying you would come to this table so I might have a chance to talk to you." The woman, whose name was Robin, told me one of the most complicated hate stories I have ever heard. Her father died when she was just a little girl. Her mother never remarried but worked very hard to give her daughter a stable home and a good education.

But the lack of a father had left an emotional vacuum in Robin which had never been filled. As a teenager, she had a tendency to reach out for male attention and affection. As a young woman, she had found herself drawn to older men. Although this had led her into some unhealthy relationships, she had always been able to get out of them before she became too involved. Then a very charming and persuasive man had led her along in a relationship which had ended in what would now be considered "date rape." She was shocked and deeply hurt, and immediately broke off the relationship, but told no one about what occurred. Ten years passed. Robin became quite an accomplished musician and held good jobs. Along the way she got married and had a family, and both she and her husband became real Christians and were active in a nearby church. After struggling with strong resentments over the rape, she had put it all out of her mind; since becoming a Christian, she had not seemed much troubled by it.

Then Robin's mother wrote of meeting a wonderful man. Although he was a bit younger, she said they got along very well. Two months later she wrote that she had married him and was happy for the first time in many *years. Naturally Robin was glad for her mother and looked forward to meeting the man. You can imagine the incredible shock when Robin's new stepfather turned out to be the man who, years ago, had sexually forced himself upon her. She wept bitterly as she described how that event's painful memories and seething resentments had been reactivated. For two years now she had been on the verge of an emotional breakdown, boiling with bitterness toward the man, and feeling mixed emotions for her mother. It had literally been consuming her until both her health and her relationship with God were being destroyed.*

Although we counseled at considerable length, not until the final healing service of the retreat was she able to let go of her hate. It was while three of us who were leaders laid hands on Robin and were praying for her that it seemed as if something was physically torn from deep inside her.

Later, Robin described the victory she had experienced. "I tried, but I couldn't release my hate, until finally in my desperation I told God I was willing for Him to take it away. And then I literally felt like some terrible black tumor had been cut out and lifted from me. I actually experienced physical pain at the time and thought I would pass out. Now I am able to forgive and accept the situation. I don't think I'll ever be close to my mother and her husband, but the hate is gone and I feel at peace in my heart." In her letters following the retreat, Robin shared that gradually her own wholeness returned and her relationships with everyone improved.

Forgiving those who have hurt us is usually difficult and can be very complex. It was certainly like that in the life of Joseph. He had been Prime Minister of Egypt for seven years now. The divine plan given to him had been put into operation. Twenty percent of the bumper crop was stored in special bins in various locations throughout the land.

Then the regular monsoon rains failed, the river began to dry up, and the parched land cracked beneath the heat. The drought extended to all the neighboring countries of that area and the famine was widespread. "And all the countries came to *Egypt to buy grain from Joseph,* because the famine was severe in all the world" (Genesis 41:57). Note my italics—

> Forgiving those who have hurt us is usually difficult and can be very complex.

Joseph now became even more than the Chief Minister of Egypt—no small honor. His name was a household word in all of that part of the world, the difference between life and death.

So it was inevitable that the good news would reach famine-ridden Canaan. "When Jacob learned that there was grain in Egypt, he said to his sons, 'Why do you just keep looking at each other?... I have heard that there is grain in Egypt. Go down there and buy some for us, so that we may live and not die'" (Genesis 42:1, 2). It doesn't look as if those selfish, irresponsible brothers had changed much, does it? Or could it be that in spite of the passing of more than twenty years, there was still an undercurrent of guilt which troubled them whenever they thought of a caravan journey to Egypt? However, finally under the prodding of their father, ten of them set out for Egypt to buy food. Jacob, with bitter memories of what happened to his other favorite son, didn't send young Benjamin along with them.

We are not going to go into all the fascinating and, at times, mysterious details of the next three chapters of Genesis, even though they read somewhat like a complicated whodunit. Our concern is with Joseph's struggle to forgive his brothers and to be reconciled with them, and the lessons this can teach us. *I am convinced that it was a genuine struggle for Joseph, and not at all like the easy and automatic response some have depicted it to be.*

First, we are told that after his marriage and during the seven good years, two sons were born to Joseph. In those days children were often given names that expressed either some historical event or their parents' feelings at the time of their birth. "Joseph named his firstborn Manasseh, and said, 'It is because God has made me forget all my trouble and all my father's household.' The second son he named Ephraim and said, 'It is because God has made me fruitful in the land of my suffering'" (Genesis 41:51-52). Those names tell us a great deal about the long and difficult process of Joseph's struggle with his own memories of his "trouble," his home sickness for his "father's household" and his "suffering." They certainly reveal his feelings toward those who had been the cause of it all.

The strongest evidence of how painful this whole experience really had been is that the writer of Genesis goes out of his way to describe in some detail the three times when Joseph, no longer able to control himself, broke down and wept (Genesis 42:24, 43:30-31; 45:1-2). In the final scene, we read, "And he wept so loudly that the Egyptians heard him, and Pharaoh's household heard about it" (Genesis 45:2). To forgive those who have hurt

> *To forgive those who have destroyed our dreams is difficult, but it is always necessary.*

us and have destroyed our dreams is usually difficult, sometimes even painful and costly; but according to the Scriptures, it is always necessary.

Jesus' Stress on Forgiving

Bishop Arthur J. Moore, the saintly bishop who commissioned Helen and me as missionaries, had an interesting way of saying something when he wanted to really emphasize it. "And now beloved, I want to say with unbecoming earnestness…" As we approach the matter of forgiveness, I want to say with unbecoming earnestness that *forgiveness is the key relational issue of the Bible.* It is also of absolutely crucial importance if we want to succeed in enemy territory. When I speak of forgiveness, I mean it in every possible sense:

- In the active voice where I am the subject of forgiveness, I forgive someone for wronging me
- In the passive voice, where I am the object of the forgiveness, I am forgiven by God and someone else for my wrongdoing
- And in the reflexive voice where I am both the subject and the object of the forgiveness, I forgive myself for my wrongdoing

In the Scripture they are all interrelated. However, as we look at the Joseph story, we shall put most of our emphasis on forgiveness in the active sense—the necessity to forgive others who have wronged us.

The stress Jesus put on forgiveness is almost shocking. *He doesn't give us any other option, if we are to be His disciples.* In what we call "The Lord's Prayer," He states, "Forgive us our debts, as we have forgiven our debtors" (Matthew 6:12). This is the only part of that prayer on which He felt the need to make any comment! "For if you forgive men when they sin against you, your heavenly Father will also forgive you. But if you do not forgive men their sins, your Father will not forgive your sins" (Matthew 6:14-15). And in Mark 11:25 we read, "And when you stand praying, if you hold anything against anyone, forgive him, so that your Father in heaven may forgive you your sins."

When Peter asked Jesus, "Lord, how many times shall I forgive my brother when he sins against me? Up to seven times?" Jesus illustrated His "seventy-times-seven" answer by giving an entire parable on the subject. The story ends by the angry master turning over the unforgiving servant to the jailers for torture and torment, until he repays all of his once-forgiven—but now fully reissued—debt. Jesus then made the application in one of the harshest statements of his entire ministry: "This is how My heavenly Father will treat each of you unless you forgive your brother from your heart" (Matthew 18:35). We can sum up our Lord's plain teachings on the subject in one short statement: "Forgive and you will be forgiven" (Luke 6:37*b*).

Thus, Jesus makes it clear that forgiving others is directly related to our being forgiven by God, and our unwillingness to forgive destroys the bridge over which God's forgiveness comes to us. Since this is such an important issue, and one about which I find much misunderstanding among Christians, I want us to look at it in considerable detail.

There are many Christians who do not understand what it means to forgive. In the name of being spiritual, they often generalize much too quickly and say, "Oh yes, of course, I've forgiven everyone who ever did anything against me." They try to jump into forgiveness with one great flying leap. This may sound good, but it doesn't work because it's unreal. It will help us to succeed in this important area if we look at the subject both negatively and positively.

> *Our unwillingness to forgive destroys the bridge over which God's forgiveness comes to us.*

What Forgiveness Is NOT

Sometimes it helps to discover what a thing is, if we first clear away what it is not.

Forgiving is not overlooking the wrong. "Oh that's all right," or "Forget it, I didn't pay any attention to it." As Christians often we think we are being super-spiritual by saying such things. This kind of blanket coverage which pretends to resolve by overlooking is just that—a blanket which covers but does not bring healing. Overlooking does not necessarily mean forgiving the person who has wronged you.

Forgiving is not excusing or whitewashing the wrong. Joseph is a good example in this regard. He said to his brothers, "As for you, you meant evil against me; but God meant it for good" (Genesis 50:20*a*, *RSV*). Most of the time we emphasize the last half of this verse, and rightly so. We are going to spend an entire chapter on the message in that half. But we must not overlook the first part. Joseph did not say to his brothers, "Well, that's okay, guys. I was just a teenager, and I know you didn't really mean anything that day you threw me down into that dry cistern at Dothan. And I know you were just playing around when you turned me over to those Midianites." How absurd that would have been! Joseph looked at his brothers with ruthless moral honesty and made no attempt to excuse or whitewash the terrible things they had done to him. He not only called a spade a spade, but even dug deep into their motivations with his spade—"You intended to harm me." One of the first steps in truly forgiving someone is to recognize the wrong and the harm they have done to you. Whitewashing temporarily covers up the hurt, but it will not result in healing or reconciliation because it is not forgiveness.

Forgiving is not psychoanalyzing the wrongdoer in order to explain away the wrong. We live in an age where we think it's helpful to analyze other people's behavior so we can understand why they do what they do. We somehow feel that if we can just figure out why the person did something to us, it will be much easier to forgive.

In the Bible, we are reminded of the mystery of God's great love for us, but we are also reminded of the mystery of iniquity or sin (2 Thessalonians 2:7, *KJV*). There is a moral stupidity about sin. It doesn't make sense. In fact, Jesus rarely called anyone a sinner, but He often called people fools or foolish. How often we hear people say, "I just can't understand how she could do that." Or, "It's crazy. He had everything. Why did he throw it all away?" Jesus recognized this when He prayed from the cross, "Father, forgive them, for they do not know what they are doing" (Luke 23:34*a*).

There *is* an element of truth in the saying, "To understand all is to forgive all." Understanding *why* may help put us on the road toward forgiveness, but understanding is not the same as forgiving. There are many times when it is utterly impossible to figure out the why of it all. Consequently, we use many of the modern labels which help to explain. "Well, you see, grandfather was an alcoholic and that made mother a terrible neurotic and"—on and on it goes. We are trying to explain in order to explain *away*. We think by doing this we are forgiving. *That is not necessarily so.* If we can't analyze the *why* of a situation, does that mean that we can't forgive?

> *Understanding is not the same as forgiving.*

This principle is particularly well illustrated by the following story. The worst case of child abuse I ever heard of was told to me by a man I counseled who had been verbally and physically abused by his mother. If you sat down and tried to conjure up ways of hurting and making a child miserable, you could not come up with more exquisite forms of cruelty. Though he was now a grown man, he sobbed with bitter rage as he told me about it. When he was four, his mother made his favorite food, peanut butter and jelly sandwiches. Only she would throw them down, open-faced, on the kitchen floor, chop them into little pieces with a butcher knife and then tell him, "Get down and eat them off the floor—like the dog you are."

What bothered him most was the fact that he had been adopted. After sharing some particularly painful memory, he would often cry out, "But why, why did she want to adopt me if she was going to treat me like that? I can't figure it out." One day I had to gently but firmly confront him with the fact that he might never be able to figure it out, and if he waited until he fully understood, he would probably never forgive her. It was a struggle, but during a long period of prayer he found the grace to forgive.

In another instance, a woman in her mid-thirties came forward and knelt at the prayer altar after I had preached a sermon on emotional healing. She wept and prayed until everyone else had left the church. Then, with bitter tears she told about being sexually used by an older brother when she was a young teenager. She cried out, "Why, why did he do that to me? How could he do it when he knew I loved him so much? What did he have in mind? If I could just understand!"

I finally stopped her painful recital, "Sister, if you are waiting to understand why he did it, you may wait a lifetime. I'm not sure even *he* would know the answer. The question now is whether you are willing to forgive him, even though you do not understand why." It wasn't easy, but she was finally able to forgive her brother "from her heart."

The need to analyze in order to understand before we forgive is especially strong among children, particularly when the wrong involves their parents. It's terribly hard to face the fact that those who are supposed to love us can actually do things which hurt us so much. And so we feel we must analyze; we think that if we understand, we have forgiven. Don't make the mistake of confusing the two.

Forgiving is not taking the blame upon ourselves. Another common mistake many Christians make is the reverse of the previous one. In this case we analyze ourselves, trying to find a legitimate excuse for the person's hurtful behavior. Joseph tried every way to soften the pain and self-incrimination which he knew the brothers would face when they recognized who he was. But taking blame on himself was not one of these ways. Though it should not be ours either, many Christians do it in the name of being spiritual and forgiving.

I remember a young lady in college whose mother had thrown her down the stairs at age three and had broken her leg. Her father had left scars on her body by using his belt buckle for "spankings." Try as I might, I could never get her to really face these wrongs. Instead she would always say, "But I must have done something terrible for that to happen. I guess I deserved it." It seemed easier for her to assume the blame than to face the terrible wrongs that they had done to her. A big part of the problem was her total misunderstanding of several Scriptures about suffering. She thought she was always to take the blame, even when others were obviously at fault. We had to carefully sort out some unhealthy theology before she came to see the truth. She was not "being a good Christian" by taking the blame, nor was she forgiving her parents.

Many marriage partners have been badly misinstructed on the matter of "authority" and "submission" in Ephesians 5, mostly by male preachers. The women who internalize this mis-instruction always take the blame, grovel, and ask for forgiveness, even when they are not in the wrong. This is not being "a good Christian wife," or following God's plan for marriage. Rather, it is unhealthy neurotic behavior and should be faced as such. It is certainly not the same as forgiveness.

The trouble with these four counterfeits, which so often pass for forgiveness, is that they simply will not work. The reason is simple: The Holy Spirit is the Spirit of Truth, and He works in our lives and relationships through truthfulness. He is the one who mediates forgiveness and He does it through truth. All of the counterfeits listed are untruthful because they are unreal. The Spirit of Truth cannot bless such exercises in unreality.

What Forgiveness IS

Having cleared away the negatives, let us now look at four essentials for truly forgiving others.

Forgiving is facing the specific wrong done to us. When Joseph finally revealed himself to his brothers, he was very specific about it all. "I am your brother, Joseph, the one you sold into Egypt" (Genesis 45:4). There was no attempt to cover up with a generalization like, "You weren't very nice to me," or "You were pretty mean to me when I was a kid." There is an important principle involved here that we often hear stressed in connection with God's forgiveness of us. We need to be specific in confessing our sins to God in order to receive His true forgiveness, and we cannot confess to God what we will not acknowledge to ourselves.

In the same way, we need to acknowledge to ourselves the specific wrong done *to* us in order to forgive the person for it. Otherwise we will make generalizations about people, give them sweeping generalizations of

100

forgiveness, and end up with hazy, confused feelings which cannot bring lasting peace. Whenever people tell me they are having battles over resentment and bitterness against someone, and then describe the problem in general terms, I always work with them until they come to grips with particulars. One way to do this is to have them write out a list of specific incidents. I always remind them that nothing is too small or too silly to include on their "hate and hurt list." The next element in forgiveness will illustrate what I mean.

We cannot confess to God what we will not acknowledge to ourselves.

Forgiveness is facing the hurt and pain resulting from the wrong done to us. Along with the specific wrongs, we must also face the specific feelings which they caused in us. The two work very closely together and we must not try to separate them. Sometimes people tell me the most terrible things without any expression of feelings—a clinical recital of the details without allowing themselves to make any emotional connection with them. They deny the pain the injury caused them. Sometimes they express a lot of emotions but deny the connection by generalizing and avoiding the particulars. The wrongs and the feelings need to be connected.

Let me list some of the most familiar and comprehensive "feeling words" people have shared with me and then some examples of how the words became related to a specific which needed their forgiving. Note that in almost every case these incidents involved someone who damaged or destroyed a dream. I suggest that you read them slowly, take the time to let your mind fill in your own personal pictures, and allow yourself to truly experience the emotions which arise from them.

Rejected—"When I was a girl of eight, desperately trying to get my father's love and attention, I gave him a birthday gift I had bought by saving every penny of my allowance for several months. He looked at it and put it on the table saying, 'Why did you get that silly thing? We've got too much junk lying around the house now.' That was a turning point for me. I stopped trying to get his love and approval and started despising him."

Humiliated—"I was on a Cub Scout camping trip, trying to earn my merit badge in basic health and hygiene. We were all outdoors brushing our teeth while the scoutmaster walked up and down watching us. When we were finished he said, 'All of you passed except Donald R. Williams.' He pronounced my full name sarcastically. 'He doesn't even know how to do something as simple as brushing his teeth. Can you imagine that?' The guys joined him in laughing hilariously. I have relived the shame of that scene a thousand times, always with bitterness toward that scoutmaster. I have a hard time not resenting any kind of kidding."

Undervalued—"As long as I can remember it was always, 'Why can't you be like Shirley?' or 'If you would just try harder, you could be just as popular as Shirley.' Or 'get as good grades,' or 'have as many dates.' You know, when my sister Shirley got pregnant in high school, I acted sorry but I was secretly glad. Isn't that awful? For once I was better than she was. It's so strange—I wanted to be like her but detested her at the same time."

Deprived or Neglected—From a man, "Both of my parents worked outside the home. I got so I dreaded coming home from school in the afternoons, especially in the winter when it was dark. To this day I am afraid of entering buildings unless they are brightly lighted. I never said anything at the time, but there was always a smoldering resentment toward my mom for not being there like the other moms."

From a wife in her forties, "My husband has literally buried himself in his work. He gets his satisfaction from his job while I've been emotionally dying on the vine. He ignores my needs for affection—even sex. It has driven me to seek it elsewhere, though I can never quite go through with an affair. I hold things together for the sake of my Christian commitment and the children, but I live with a slow burn toward him all the time."

Outraged—"My dad was unpredictable and irrational. He'd get some crazy idea and force it on the rest of the family. Or he'd get mad at one kid and punish us all, saying we had probably planned it together. When he was in a good mood we could do anything—terrible things—and he'd just laugh. Then for some minor mistake he'd lay it on us with a heavy spanking or a major time of grounding. The punishment never seemed to fit the crime. Nothing made sense, and I got worn out from walking on eggshells. It just wasn't fair. To this day I get filled with rage whenever I see injustice."

Diminished—"I got so I could handle the daily barrage of ordinary belittling and put-downs, but it was the spiritual ones that finally broke me. One night during my high school days, I went forward at the church. I was fully repentant and earnest about my decision to follow Christ, regardless of what the other girls did. At breakfast Mom said sarcastically, 'Well, I'll believe it when I see a real change in your life.' I left the meal, went upstairs and said to myself, 'There's no way I can ever prove to Mom that I sincerely want to live for God, and if I can't prove it to her, how can I ever prove it to God?' I was filled with bitterness, and from that morning it was downhill all the way."

Abused—"I was a strong athletic guy and got so I could handle the beatings—I still have some of the scars. It was the verbal abuse, the sharp, cruel words that cut the deepest. The whole bit about how much trouble I'd been before I was born and since I was born, and worst of all, 'I wish you'd never been born,' has left the most painful scars. Whenever I see a mother or dad hugging their child, I inwardly cry and get filled with hate."

Betrayed—"We gave our son everything good parents should: Sunday School, church, summer youth camps, and family devotions. We sacrificed to give him good clothes and all the paraphernalia of teenagers so he wouldn't feel left out. We took him for practices and attended all the games he played in. Now we discover he's been on drugs and alcohol for quite a while. We feel terribly betrayed; we're very angry at him and have a hard time not being bitter toward him."

Or, "I can't believe it. My husband/wife had an affair with my best friend. Everybody knew it before I did. I feel so betrayed by both of them."

Or, "I loved my grandpa so much. He'd give me candy and stuff. And then he asked me to do all those things with him, told me it made me special and not to tell anyone about our little love secret. How could he betray me like that?"

Abandoned—"I couldn't believe it. I just came home from work one day and she was gone, and the kids were all alone, scared, and crying. I didn't know where she was. It took me months to find out she was with someone else up in Michigan. I was just plain abandoned. It was devastating."

Forgiveness is facing our resentments. In Ephesians 4:25-31, Paul seems to indicate a gradation in levels of ill will. He begins with *anger* which has been left to fester, then *unwholesome talk*, then *bitterness, rage, brawling, slander, malice.* Before we can truly forgive, we must have the courage to face our real feelings toward the person. Sometimes I ask, "Would *rage* or even *hate* be too strong a word?" Often people reply, "I'm ashamed to admit it, but that's the way I feel." Don't deny it, hide it, or dismiss it with a Christian cliché or a pious-sounding Bible verse.

One counselee did just that. He would not face the truth, but kept dismissing deep family hurts with, "But doesn't the Bible say that our greatest enemies are the members of our own household?" (Matthew 10:36). He couldn't seem to understand why there was no permanent healing or peace in his heart.

An important principle of Biblical psychology is involved here: If you bury the hurts, you bury the hates. And if you bury the hurts and the hates, then you bury the possibility of healing.

Forgiveness is facing the cross of Christ. Now we have reached the place where we have a real choice—to forgive or not to forgive. I don't mean to suggest that everyone actually has to sit down and say, "I am going to take steps one, two, three and forgive so-and-so for such-and-such." Some of the steps may be compressed and telescoped together. However, the journey to forgiveness will always involve these steps in one form or another.

In any case, after we have faced the wrongs and felt the hurts and admitted the resentments, there is only one place to which we can go—the cross of Christ. Paul ends the Ephesian passage to which we have already referred by turning our faces toward Calvary. "Be kind and compassionate to one another, forgiving each other, just as in Christ God forgave you" (Ephesians 4:32).

Do not pass over this lightly, for there is deep theological reasoning behind Paul's plea. Paul is saying that when God forgave us our sins through Christ's death, it was because God in Christ took onto Himself and into Himself the guilt, the punishment, and the shame of our sins. These should have been ours, because we deserved to suffer for them. Instead, God took them into His very own being and by suffering for them was able to forgive us without overlooking or whitewashing our sins.

To a much lesser degree, but in exactly the same way, when we forgive someone who has wronged and hurt us, we are taking the pain and shame they deserve to suffer onto and into ourselves. This is why all forgiveness, divine or human, involves suffering love. The only place in all the universe where we humans are enabled to have that kind of suffering love is beneath the cross of Jesus. The golden rule of forgiveness then is not, "Do unto others as you would have them do unto you," but "Do unto others as God in Christ has done unto you."

One of my most beloved spiritual mentors was Dr. E. Stanley Jones. In his book, *Christ and Human Suffering*, he tells a moving story to illustrate this truth.

A government official in India told me how he became a changed man... He said that he took his first step into immorality when he went to Europe to study. He left behind him a pure, innocent, trusting wife—the soul of honor. When he came back from Europe, instead of turning from his unfaithfulness he continued his double life. The purity and trust of his wife stabbed him like a knife, until the time came when he could hold the guilty secret no longer. He determined to tell his wife, but he was inwardly afraid—she would probably leave him, or wither him with her anger. But one day he decided to face it, so he called her into his room, shut the door, and began to unfold the whole wretched story. As the meaning of what he was saying dawned upon her, she turned as pale as death, staggered against the wall and leaned there with the tears trickling down her cheeks. As he stood watching he saw his sin crucifying his wife—her pure love was being tortured on the cross of his sin. "That moment," he said, "I saw the meaning of the cross of Christ. I saw from her lesser cross the meaning of the greater cross. And when she said through her tears that she would not leave me, but would help me back to a new life, I felt the offer of a new beginning in the cross of Christ, and from that moment I was a new man."[1]

Rosamond E. Herklots expresses this truth in her beautiful hymn, "Forgive Our Sins As We Forgive."

> "Forgive our sins as we forgive,"
>   You taught us, Lord, to pray;
> But You alone can grant us grace
>   To live the words we say.
>
> How can Your pardon reach and bless
>   The unforgiving heart
> That broods on wrongs and will not let
>   Old bitterness depart?
>
> In blazing light Your cross reveals
>   The truth we dimly knew:
> What trivial debts are owed to us,
>   How great our debt to You?

9

FORGIVING—GOD'S PART AND OURS

*D*enny was obviously very upset when he sat down before me. "I just don't understand," he said with almost a tinge of anger in his voice. "I went to a retreat two weeks ago and the Spirit forced me to face up to the fact that I had not truly forgiven Mike, a guy who wronged me terribly several years ago. Though it was a struggle, God gave me the grace to really forgive him. And I've had wonderful peace in my heart since then. But within the last few days, a lot of those old feelings have come back and I've been overwhelmed by them. That surprises me. I guess I didn't really forgive him. I thought I had. Maybe I'll have to do it all over again; but to be honest with you, I'm afraid it's not going to work this time either. I'm quite discouraged about it."*

Although the names and circumstances differ, I have heard that same story from hundreds of people. This is such a common experience for many Christians and one of those areas where we can suffer defeat. Therefore, let us look in further detail at the subject so we will not fall prey to "the father of lies." This is one of those important areas where we need to know the truth and be set free from unnecessary confusion, guilt, and condemnation.

We must first make sure that we understand the division of labor involved in forgiving others. There is a human part, something only we can do; and there is a divine part, something only *God* can do. There is also an area where the human and the divine work together in mutual cooperation. This division of labor means we cannot do God's part and God cannot do our part. We get into trouble if we try to do what only God can do. We get into equal trouble if we ask God to do what He has ordained that only we can do. The human part is the crisis of our will. The divine part is the process of changing our feelings. Let us carefully sort out these different areas of work and responsibility.

Our Part—The Crisis of Our Will

The crisis of our will simply means our willingness to forgive the wrongdoer. I speak of it as a crisis, for even though reaching the place of willingness may involve a lengthy process, there does come a time and a place where we have to make a definite crisis decision as to whether or not we will forgive. Let me clarify what I mean by explaining the process leading up to the crisis.

It is important that we begin where we are, not where we think we ought to be. If we can't start at home plate, we can begin at first base, or at second base. We may even have to start out in center field. When I have asked people if they are willing to forgive, many have replied, "I know I ought to forgive. I really want to, but I'll have to be honest with you. The hurt is so great that I don't think I'm quite willing to forgive right now." When that is the case I thank them for their honesty and then ask another question, "Are you willing to be made willing?" This is not just some fancy play on words. It recognizes where we really are, and moves the question back to a prior level. It tries to start from where we are to help move us toward the place of decision. It is asking God's grace to help us get to where we are willing to be made willing, even at the cost of greater pain. Thank God He is wonderfully patient and gracious with us, and honors the sincerity of our desire in the midst of our struggle.

> *It is important that we begin where we are, not where we think we ought to be.*

There is a lovely incident in the New Testament which has relevance to us in such a situation (Mark 9:14-29). It's the story of the father who brought his son to Jesus for healing. At first he was not quite sure Jesus wanted to heal him. Jesus in effect said, "Of course, I want to heal him, and everything is possible to those who believe. Do you believe that I can?" The man, grappling with his imperfect faith, cried out, "I believe; help my unbelief" (Mark 9:24, *RSV*). Then Jesus said, "Well, I'm sorry, but it's obvious you don't have a pure enough faith to really believe. I tell you what. Why don't you take your boy and go back home. Then, work on your faith for the next couple of weeks. And when you've got your act together and think you have a perfect faith and you really do believe, then bring him back and I'll see what I can do for him."

No, No, No! Maybe that's what we would have said, but not Jesus. Instead, He accepted the father's desire to believe, honored his imperfect but determined faith, and healed his son. Jesus, as it were, recognized his willingness to be willing to believe, and acted on that. In the same way, Jesus will honor our struggles and the set of our sails in the direction of forgiveness. The moment we say, "Lord, I'm not quite willing to forgive, but I'm willing for You to make me willing whatever the cost," all of God's enabling grace is ours. He is faithful and will work with us to bring us step by step to the place where we can do our part, where we can progressively say, "Lord, I am willing to be made willing ... I am willing to forgive ... I will to forgive ... Lord, I do forgive!"

In order to help people to the crisis of decision, I often ask them, "If God were to walk into this office right now and offer to give you a whole set of new feelings toward that person, would you accept those feelings? Would you take those feelings and begin to exercise them, use them, allow them to become your own feelings? Or would you hang on to the old ones and insist on keeping them?" Usually they reply, "Since you put it that way, I understand what you mean by my part in this transaction. Yes, I am willing for God to make me willing."

Willingness to forgive means we will not hold on to the old feelings but will accept new ones. Please note that I have not said anything about the content of the feelings themselves, only about our decision to forgive the person. From the human standpoint our only responsibility is the will to forgive, meaning the willingness to forgive.

God's Part—The Process of Changing Our Feelings

"But don't I somehow have to get over those terrible feelings toward that person?" No, that's God's part in the matter, not yours. We need to get off God's turf. The reason the Lord says, "Vengeance is mine, I will repay" (Romans 12:19*b*, *RSV*) is because when we try to avenge ourselves or get even, we are getting on God's turf. We are trying to exercise a prerogative that belongs only to God: We are attempting to take things into our own hands and make our business what is strictly His. In the same way, when we say we are going to forgive someone and then try to change our own feelings toward them, we are also getting onto God's turf. We are breaking into the divine division of labor and trying to do what only God can do.

In fact, after a lifetime of counseling, I am convinced that we fallen human beings cannot really change our feelings about anything—resentments, jealousies, addictions, attachments, affairs, whatever it may be. So what do we do? Do we just say that we're sorry we feel this way, but there's nothing we can do about it? Not at all.

Whatever the issue, it comes down to a place of decision, a crisis of the will, where we decide whether or not to allow God to change them. That's our part—will we give God permission to change our feelings? We may have to reiterate the decision again and again. At first we may have to do it every hour on the hour. "Yes, Lord, that is my will. I will not hold onto the old feelings; I will accept the new ones." But the actual changing of the feelings is God's responsibility.

> *"You can always send your will on ahead by lightning express, but your feelings usually come later by slow freight."*

There is a big difference between the two in regard to time or timing. As a teenage Christian, I heard some of the great preachers of that day. It was the era of the railroads and many of their illustrations were taken from them. I will always remember a marvelous word picture Dr. Henry Clay Morrison used. He would say, "You can always send your will on ahead by lightning express, but your feelings usually come later by slow freight."

Yes, our decision can be made in a short time. Sometimes, if we are ready, it can be done in a crisis instant. The changing of the feelings, though, is a process and usually takes a much longer time to accomplish. Sometimes God seems to peel off layer after layer of feelings as old memories return and new ones arise. All of a sudden we remember some other wrongs, or another picture appears on the screen of our minds and former wounds are reopened. Each time we obediently reiterate our original decision to forgive and we release these fresh hurts to God, He keeps replacing the old feelings with new ones in an ongoing process.

A most dramatic illustration of this took place in the life of the saintly Corrie ten Boom. She told this electrifying story when she held evangelistic services in our church in Bangalore, India, in 1961. After World War II was over, Corrie had traveled to many different countries telling about her Holocaust experiences. She had always stressed that God had long ago given her the grace to forgive her torturers. Finally she returned to speak in Germany itself. One night after she had spoken at a church service in Munich, she was shocked to see in the congregation the very S.S. officer who had stood guard at the shower room door in the processing center at Ravensbruck Prison.

It was the first time she had actually met one of those wretched, cruel jailers. She said that she was suddenly ambushed by painful memories— the heaps of dirty clothing, the humiliation of her nakedness, the roomful of jeering men, her sister Betsie's pallid face. A flood of vengeful feelings boiled up within her once again. She could forgive the others, maybe, but not this man. And then, to her horror, the man came up to her, his face all aglow. "O Fraulein," he said, "thank you for your message. I believe what you said, that God has forgiven me and washed all my sins away." He reached out his hand to shake hers, but the hateful feelings were too strong. She could not even raise her hand. She felt nothing, not even the slightest emotion of pity. How could she shake his hand? It would be completely phony. But God kept whispering in her heart, "Just put out your hand, Corrie, that's all." Finally, breathing a desperate prayer for strength, she reached out and took his hand. When she did, the most amazing thing happened. It was as though an electric current flowed through her shoulder and arm and into her hand. The rage melted and a deep feeling of forgiving love welled up inside her! She said, "I had to obey God and put out my hand. He did the rest!"

I think it was somewhat like that with Joseph. He had certainly forgiven his brothers many years before. We know that for sure, because he could never have survived the slavery, the injustice, the imprisonment, and the disillusionment, if he had not had a forgiving spirit. But, like Corrie ten Boom, *he had not seen those wretched brothers face to face for over twenty years!* So when he did, he had to deal with a mind full of bitter memories, and a heart full of painful feelings, along with eyes overflowing with bitter tears. Once again he reiterated his full forgiveness of them for the evil things they intentionally did to him.

This is the lesson we too must learn—to obediently maintain our will to forgive even when feelings overwhelm us. In this connection, and perhaps most important of all, God does not want us to feel guilt or condemnation about the process, regardless of how long it may take. We should only rejoice and be thankful for the way His love is slowly but surely filling in all the crannies and crevices of our hearts. Any feelings of self-recrimination are not from God; they are coming from Satan who is truly the accuser of God's children. It is a demonic attempt to call unclean what God has called clean.

Here are some practical suggestions, five important R's for resisting times of attack which come through recurring feelings.

- *Recall* their source—Satan, the father of lies
- *Reiterate* your will to forgive
- *Refuse* to allow guilt or condemnation a place in your heart
- *Remember* God is faithful and will continue to change your feelings
- *Rejoice* that God is pleased with you every step of the way

We have considered the general division of labor in forgiving others. Now I want to share some of the particulars which I have discovered to be important ingredients of forgiveness.

Assuming Responsibility

There is an inseparable connection between forgiving others and assuming responsibility for our lives. Forgiveness and responsibility are two sides of the same coin. God taught me this the hard way—in my own personal life.

In my early Christian life, for many more years than I like to admit, I felt as if I never made a mistake or failed at anything I did. Not literally, of course. Yes, I blew it, I failed, I made terrible mistakes, and I fell. But not really, because it wasn't *really* me. Every time I failed or fell or missed the mark, there was a little photoelectric cell that automatically turned on the current inside of my brain. I could almost hear it go *ping* when it switched on. And a light came on, and then a tiny voice inside me whispered, "That's okay, David. Sure, you blew it, you made a mistake, but don't worry about it. You wouldn't have done that if you had had a different mother." I didn't have to flip a switch—it came on by itself. It was fully automatic, like the doors at the grocery store which open or close when we get near them. I'm ashamed to say I lived with that and believed it for many years. It was a down-filled comforter, a built-in excuse blanket that cushioned me whenever I fell.

But when God led me into my own personal experience of deep inner healing, I had to wade through the waters of forgiveness. This little mental exercise was one of the first things He pointed out to me, "David, that's got to go. From now on it's just you and Me, with no one to blame. You must assume full responsibility for your life—your choices, your attitudes, and actions. From now on they're all yours."

In the beginning, I found that terribly difficult, for the old automatic light and voice would switch on like clockwork. I had to deliberately turn them off and break a habit of many years. I had to intentionally work at owning my choices and assuming full responsibility for my life. This was a vital part of the forgiving process.

There are multitudes of Christians who refuse to fully forgive from their hearts (Matthew 18:35), because they know if they do they will have to take full responsibility for their lives and stop playing the blame game. Counselees often tell me they will have to "let someone off the hook" if they forgive them.

I will always remember the way Rod visualized the expression. He worked in the meat department of a large supermarket. He confessed deep-seated resentments against his brothers who had not in-

> *Assuming his share of responsibility for the broken relationships was the essential ingredient to forgiveness and reconciliation.*

cluded him in the family reunions, and then asked me, "Have you ever been in a large freezer like the one at the back of our meat department?" I told him that I had only seen them on TV, but I had a pretty good idea of what they were like. "Well, ours is really big. It's filled with sides of beef and hams and other cuts of meat. They're all hanging from the ceiling on big hooks. Recently, as I thought of my brothers whom I resented, God said to me, 'It's like you've got them all cut up and hanging on hooks in the deep freeze in your heart. You need to forgive them, and take them off those hooks and let them come back into your life.'" Rod added, "I haven't been able to get that picture out of my mind. I can just see them impaled on my hooks of hate. Pray with me, Pastor. I need to forgive them and let them off the hook."

Previously, I had always thought of bitterness and hate in terms of heat—the slow burn, boiling water, or an erupting volcano with red-hot lava running down its sides. This picture of people hanging from hooks in a deep freeze, however, was so vivid that it has never left my mind. I am happy to report that the Holy Spirit poured warm *agapé* love into Rod. This thawed out his frigid heart, and gave him grace to let his brothers off the hook and restore them back into his life once again. After it was all over, he admitted that assuming his share of responsibility for the broken relationships was the essential ingredient to forgiveness and reconciliation.

In the summer of 1989, Helen and I had the great privilege of minister-ing to the Methodist Church in Estonia. The only Methodists left in the Soviet Union, they suffered terrible persecution from the time that Stalin took over the Baltic States. Many have both physical and emotional scars from their years in Siberian concentration camps. Since the Russians did not allow Estonian pastors out of the country for training, Asbury Semi-nary has been sending professors over to train them. I went largely to preach and give seminars on counseling. One day the Spirit led me to put aside my planned lectures and talk on responsibility and forgiveness. The response was overwhelming. Pastors and people wept and prayed, confess-ing their hurts and bitterness.

Afterward, the superintendent of the church said to me, "We never thought about this before. We have been forgiving our enemies all these years and trying to keep hate out of our hearts. But God spoke to us today and we are going to have to change our whole attitude; for over forty years we've blamed everything on the Russians. It's been our excuse for anything that went wrong. I see that we must stop that, truly forgive, and take full responsibility for ourselves and the future of the church." It was a moving experience and totally of the Spirit, since I knew nothing about this particular aspect of the problem. It confirmed on a large scale what I had previously experienced only in the lives of individuals—that forgiveness and responsibility go hand in hand.

Is there someone you are afraid to forgive because you know that if you do it means no more blaming? That you would then have to take full responsibility for your life? Often we cannot disown our resentments until we own our responsibilities. Until we do, we cannot succeed in enemy territory.

Resentment Barrels and Paper Shredders

After the crisis decision to forgive, it is helpful to have some imaginary picture which visualizes the process of God changing our feelings. So in my mind I had what I called my "resentment barrel" to take care of any recurring feelings of resentment. I pictured the cross of Jesus and across the arms of the cross was Ephesians 4:32 in abbreviated form, "Be kind and compassionate, forgiving as God forgave you." Then underneath the cross I had a big round metal drum or barrel. Every time some of the old feelings came, I would reiterate my will to forgive, look at the cross and dump the feelings into the barrel.

I remember preaching about this many years ago. A lady came up and said she appreciated the sermon but didn't think much of my resentment barrel. "I'm not sure I've ever seen a barrel," she said rather dourly. Since I knew she was battling bitterness, I told her to ask the Spirit to help her find her own visual aid which would be meaningful for her. She wasn't too enthusiastic about the idea. The next day at work her boss told her that too much paper had piled up during the last few months and the entire office needed cleaning out. He said, "I want you to go through the files, sort out what we don't need, and run it through the paper shredder. Then I'll have it all carted away. I can't stand the mess any longer."

As she was carrying out his orders, the Holy Spirit whispered to her, "That's exactly what you need to do. You need to run your old feelings through a paper shredder and get all that old stuff cleaned out of your heart." The next Sunday she shared with me how God had provided her with just the right imagery. For a long time after that she would occasionally say to me with a smile, "I had to run my paper shredder this week—at high speed too!" Only God and I knew what she meant.

Through the years people have shared all manner of mental images they have found helpful as God continued the process of getting rid of the old feelings: trenches, pits, and landfills to bury them in, oceans and lakes to sink them in, various forms of furnaces to burn them in, and laser beams and Star Wars weapons to disintegrate them out of existence. Me? I'm still back in the dark ages with my resentment barrel. I still find it a very present help in the time of troubling emotions.

Forgiving and Being Forgiven

Up to this point we have concentrated exclusively on forgiveness in the active voice—forgiving those who have wronged us. We have done this because Jesus put such a great emphasis upon our willingness to forgive as a key factor in our being forgiven. I've learned from experience how closely the two are related and how the flow of forgiveness can go in either direction. I have seen several unsaved persons for whom the act of forgiving became the instrument of their own forgiveness and salvation.

A woman wrote me about seeing my book *Healing of Memories* in a secular bookstore. She was not a Christian and was turned off by its religious back cover copy. She was about to put it down, but decided to look at the table of contents. Since she was a victim of sexual abuse by a close relative, her attention was captured by the chapter on the healing of sexual traumas. She bought the book and began to read, but became very angry when it asked her to forgive her victimizer. She continued to read, but kept thinking she could never forgive him—in fact, ought not to forgive him. She'd been carrying her murderous hate for so long it had actually caused her physical ailments. She suddenly remembered her doctor had once asked if there was "anything eating on her that maybe she needed to resolve." She decided she would force herself to forgive—but didn't know how she could possibly do it.

She was completely unable then to explain what happened in the next hour, when she began to experience release from years of hatred and a deep sense that God loved her very much and wanted to be a true Father to her. It was the beginning of a genuine conversion experience and a changed life. As she forgave she found herself being forgiven, loved, and transformed without ever directly asking for it.

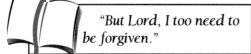

> *"But Lord, I too need to be forgiven."*

There are scores of times when something like this happens.

When we are praying with people, they are often torn with wracking pain as they face their hurts and struggle to find grace to forgive. Often, right in the middle of the prayer to forgive someone else, they suddenly stop. After what can be a rather long pause, they will say, "But Lord, I too need to be forgiven. Sure they hurt me very much, but I responded in all the wrong ways. I have hated and wanted to get even and I need to be forgiven for that. O God, forgive me." When they decide to forgive, the Spirit shows them their own need to be forgiven.

Once in a healing seminar we were having a talk-back session after my message. A distinguished, white-haired man in his eighties began to share. "I know what you're talking about. There were only two children in our family. I was the older of two brothers and it was like in Jesus' parable. I had a younger brother who broke my parents' hearts and ruined our family's good reputation in the community. I grew to hate him for what I saw him do to my wonderful parents. And this went on for almost forty years. But then he got very sick and he came back home a broken man. He repented and turned to Christ, and we all forgave him and were reconciled as a family before he died. I forgave him, I really did. But you said today that we needed to be forgiven for our hate. I'd never realized that before today, but I see that I do need to be forgiven for those years of hate." And that dear old man, so highly respected in that community, humbled himself and asked the group to lay hands on him and pray for him. Before it was over, we were all weeping together as God washed him in His forgiving love.

Yes, we need to forgive, but let us remember that *we also need to be forgiven.* Jesus stressed how closely the two are woven together. It's not that God is unwilling to forgive us until we forgive others; rather, that He is unable to forgive us, or perhaps that we are unable to experience His forgiveness without offering our willingness to forgive. I've always found each affects and is, in turn, affected by the other. It is not only "Forgive and you will be forgiven" (Luke 6:37*b*), but also forgive as you have been forgiven (Ephesians 4:32).

Forgiving Ourselves

There is another aspect of forgiveness: forgiving ourselves. This may be the hardest of all. We often see this in dramatic form among those whose sense of guilt is so great it keeps them from receiving the Gospel, the good news of forgiveness, in any way.

On November 11, 1976, I watched as ABC television news interviewed two condemned criminals. One was X. L. White, a convicted murderer who had killed three people in McKinney, Texas. During the interview he said, "I'm not going to ask anyone for forgiveness. I don't deserve it."

The other was Gary Gilmore, convicted murderer in the Utah State Prison. He refused to speak but nodded as the prison chaplain expressed Gilmore's feelings. "He is not suicidal, or mentally unbalanced at all. He knows exactly what he is doing. He feels very guilty for his crime and wants to make an atonement for his sin. He wants to die."

A few days later, Gilmore was executed by a firing squad, the first death sentence to be carried out in many years. How sad, when God Himself has written in blood on the old rugged cross, "Your sin has been forgiven and your iniquity has been taken away." Gilmore's desire is sadly understandable from this point alone: He totally refused the mercy and grace of God.

It is also sad, and difficult to understand, that vast numbers of Christians go through life saying, "Yes, I know God has forgiven me, and I've forgiven those who wronged me, but there are some things in my life for which I just cannot forgive myself." We go on flagellating ourselves, doing our penance of perpetual regret, never fully enjoying our forgiveness, and living at half-strength.

Here is the perfect place to return to the story of Joseph forgiving his brothers. In Genesis 45:5 we find one of the most amazing scenes in the whole incredible drama. Knowing that his brothers were going to have a very difficult time accepting his forgiveness, that it would be hard for them to forgive themselves, Joseph—in an act of unbelievable unselfishness— went out of his way to comfort them. He said to them, "Do not be distressed and do not be angry with yourselves for selling me here." He was actually more concerned about how they were going to feel than about how he was feeling! However, in spite of all his efforts, those poor brothers couldn't quite believe it—it was just too good to be true. Consequently, seventeen years later (Genesis 47:28), after their father Jacob died and had been buried, they once again struggled with their guilt, sure that Joseph would now take revenge upon them (Genesis 50:15-17). Joseph was so shocked by their lack of trust in him that he wept (Genesis 50:17), and once again reiterated his forgiveness of them saying, "'...Don't be afraid. I will provide for you and your children.' And he reassured them and spoke kindly to them" (Genesis 50:21).

Before you and I criticize the behavior of those unbelieving brothers, let's take a good look in the mirror and see if this isn't exactly the way we often treat God. With all of His promises by which He assures us of our full and total forgiveness, we still can't quite believe it. Long after our initial salvation, we still may not forgive ourselves, but continue punishing ourselves with self-accusations, self-punishment, and even self-atonement.

This is yet another place where, standing under the cross of Christ, we need to make a definite decision to forgive ourselves and ask God to change our feelings toward ourselves. Just as Joseph wept over his brothers' continued self-flagellation, God is grieved at our failure to forgive ourselves.

Forgiveness and Reconciliation

The Joseph story highlights an important distinction between forgiveness and reconciliation. Christians get into a lot of difficulty when they assume the two are the same thing. They are not, and we need to carefully sort out the important difference.

Joseph had forgiven his brothers many years ago. As we saw in chapter 8, for example, the names he gave his children indicated that he had experienced a genuine healing of his most painful memories. He had *forgiven* them, but he had not yet been *reconciled* to them. For this he had to wait for more than twenty years, until finally "he threw his arms around his brother Benjamin and wept, and Benjamin embraced him, weeping. And he kissed all his brothers and wept with them. Afterwards his brothers talked with him" (Genesis 45:14-15).

To forgive those who wrong and hurt us is one thing; to be reconciled with them is another. When we forgive, the walls that we have erected and which have kept us apart are broken down. As far as we are concerned, we are now free to go to them and be reconciled with them. In most instances, when we offer God our willingness to forgive, He also asks us to offer Him our willingness to go to the persons and be reconciled. For this reconciliation to take place, they need our forgiveness, and we too will need theirs. Asking for forgiveness is not an easy thing to do, and requires humility and grace on our part; but in the majority of life's simpler situations, we can forgive our wrongdoers, ask their forgiveness for our wrong feelings toward them, and the broken relationships can be restored.

> *To forgive those who wrong and hurt us is one thing; to be reconciled with them is another.*

Jesus takes this a step further in the Sermon on the Mount (Matthew 5:23-24), when He tells us to take the initiative for reconciliation, *even when other persons have something against us.* We are to go to them and do our best to remove all the barriers between us. In Matthew 18:15-17 Jesus gives some detailed instructions for confronting those who have sinned against us:

> "If your brother sins against you, go and show him his fault,
> just between the two of you. If he listens to you, you have won
> your brother over. But if he will not listen, take one or two
> others along, so that 'every matter may be established by the
> testimony of two or three witnesses.' If he refuses to listen to
> them, tell it to the church; and if he refuses to listen even to the
> church, treat him as you would a pagan or a tax collector."

Jesus is realistic enough to tell us not to expect success every time we do this. Yet, it is after this that Jesus gives us the Parable of the Unmerciful Servant which makes one thing crystal clear. We are always required to forgive from our hearts. As Christians we are not left any other option (Matthew 18:35).

However, Jesus knows that though we must always forgive, there is no guarantee that there will always be reconciliation. We Christians put ourselves under a terrible load of guilt by trying to have a standard higher than our Lord. One of our evangelical myths is this: If we fully forgive people, and do all we can to bring about reconciliation with them, they will always reciprocate with forgiveness and reconciliation, and from then on everything will be all right between us. In the simpler situations of life, it may work out that way.

The trouble is that life is not always that simple. Forgiveness is sometimes a one-way street. Reconciliation must always be a two-way street.

I have heard many sermons and seminars which do not make this distinction. They overload sincere Christians with impossible demands and unrealistic hopes. When those Christians, after forgiving their wrongdoers, try to follow through by attempts at confrontation and restoration, they run into a spiritual chain-saw massacre. I have seen great damage done on all sides by this, including some marriages and family relationships which have been completely destroyed.

In the Sermon on the Mount, the Jesus who told us to go to our brother also said, "...Do not throw your pearls to pigs. If you do, they may trample

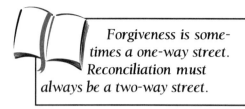

Forgiveness is sometimes a one-way street. Reconciliation must always be a two-way street.

them under their feet, and then turn and tear you to pieces" (Matthew 7:6). Prayerfully and carefully, we must find the balance between these two injunctions.

Life holds many incredibly complex situations regarding forgiving and being reconciled. We must face the fact that there are some no-win situations where our forgiveness may always remain a one-way street. In other cases, we may have to wait a long time before there can be the two-way street of reconciliation. My point is this. Don't rush from a sense of guilt or inner compulsion into confrontation and attempted reconciliation. Slow it down, and wait on the Lord. Make sure you are on His schedule and His timing, not yours. When in doubt, seek counsel from wise and more mature heads than yours.

It took twenty years of waiting for Joseph to be reconciled and restored to his brothers. Are you thinking that was forced upon him by circumstances over which he had no choice? Even that is only a partial truth. The first thirteen years he had no choice, but what about the last seven? Why did he make no attempt to get in touch with his family during the seven years he was Prime Minister of Egypt and could have easily done so? I believe Joseph was waiting for God's *kairos* time—the right time, the ripe time, the "fullness of time."

A good share of my counseling is with people who have been the victims of other people's sins—mates and children of alcoholics, children of broken homes, the physically and sexually abused, those whose marriages have been broken by infidelity and battering, and those who have suffered through other complex situations. After helping them to forgive their victimizers, I usually spend a long time on the next step. Just as Christ always requires our willingness to forgive, He also requires our willingness for reconciliation. That does not guarantee, however, that it is always possible or advisable. We spend much time praying together, offering our willingness, but waiting for the Holy Spirit's direction as to action and timing. To use Hannah Whitehall Smith's famous phrase, we pray "the prayer of relinquishment," leaving the matter in God's hands for future direction. We want to remain prayerfully sensitive to the Spirit's guidance, but resolutely resistant to Satan's attempt to make us feel guilty or pressure us into unwise action.

In my book *Putting Away Childish Things*, I shared the story of Irene. Irene came to me for help while she was in college. Her deepest problem was the struggle over deep resentments against her alcoholic father who had sexually abused her as a teenager. During our prayer time together God had wonderfully healed her memories and enabled her to fully forgive him. Due to all the complex family circumstances, we both felt it was best to wait on the Lord for any future directions. She passed into the stream of outgoing students and I heard from her only occasionally. Then came a four-page letter. Her father had taken seriously ill and had asked to see her before he died. Though convinced it was the Spirit's leading, she made the long trip in fear and hesitation. Here are a few paragraphs from her letter.

I wasn't sure how I would feel about Daddy—whether my emotions had really been healed as I trusted they were, or whether when coming into close physical proximity I would still feel that wave of nausea, so all the words of love and concern, even though they came from my heart, would have to be forced through my lips ....

The two weeks I was there were fantastic. I could almost feel the Lord hugging me close to Him, with His arms around me, guiding everything I said and did. It was a beautiful, unforgettable experience that I praise the Lord for. I wouldn't have missed it for anything! I was filled with His special joy and peace. Outside of Christ, I would have been a nervous wreck and no help to anyone.

When I saw Daddy there seemed to be an instant rapport and understanding between us, and with honest and joyful love I threw my arms around his frail, thin body, kissed him, and told him I loved him. He had tears streaming down his face. He knew and I knew that everything in the past was forgiven and washed in the blood of the Lamb. There was healing and wholeness and unspoken understanding. My heart soared! The healing and love for which I had trusted the Lord so long ago was mine, not just when I was far enough away from the problem to be able to accept it in theory, but right there in Daddy's arms.

The rest of the letter describes how she had the privilege of helping lead her father to Christ during the final days of his life. Irene's forgiveness had to wait almost ten years before it could become reconciliation.

But the best part of the story is what followed. In the years following this incident, she hesitantly but prayerfully began to share her story, at first with individual women, then in small groups which grew larger and larger. For the past few years, she has had a worldwide ministry to incest victims. She is one of God's healed helpers. Because she forgave and then waited for God's timing, He was able to take that which was meant to be evil and turn it "for good to accomplish what is now being done, the saving of many lives" (Genesis 50:20*b*).

It is to this great thought we now turn in the life of Joseph. It is the final chapter in God's plan of salvation—His power to harness evil and make it work to accomplish His purposes for our good and His glory.

10

THE 50/20 VISION OF THE DREAMER

I am a science-fiction fan. When I was a kid I loved to read the comics about Buck Rogers, and later the more serious short stories and novels; now I enjoy watching science fiction on TV. One of the most common literary devices of science fiction is the time machine. This gadget conveniently enables one to move backward or forward in time and to become a part of the lives of people in the past or the future. The hit movie *Back to the Future* used this idea with a fascinating plot: a young man went back to the time long before he was born, when his parents were youngsters in high school and were just courting each other.

I want us to imagine that we have somehow gotten into a time machine and have been propelled back several thousands of years. We are alive just after the teenage Joseph has been sold to the Midianite slave traders. It's the first night of the journey to Egypt and the Midianite caravan has made camp. The evening meal is over and has been topped off by a generous drink of wine. All are sleeping soundly in their tents: everyone except Joseph, that is. Being an extremely clever and self-confident young man, he is just pretending to be asleep. Watch him now. We can hardly believe what we are seeing. His captors have loosened the chains which bound him so he could get some sleep, and he has somehow been able to free himself from them. He is actually trying to escape from those dreadful men. They haven't traveled very far, and Joseph is an unusually strong young man who knows this area of the country like the back of his hand. He calculates that he can be back to Dothan by the next night and stay there with some distant relatives who would then help him get home.

Watch him now as he quietly crawls out of the tent and creeps along the edge of the camp. Uh-oh, what's this? A scrawny, yellow dog spots him and begins to bark. If it keeps up, the men will be awakened and they will recapture him.

Now this is the fun of science fiction. We are right there but completely invisible, so Joseph can't see us and neither can that lousy dog. We see an unused tent peg lying on the ground. Quick as a flash, we pick it up and smash that dog in the head.

There is silence once again. Joseph waits until the stirring Midianites turn over and go back to sleep. Then he stealthily slips into the night and makes his escape. Within a few days he is back home. There is an awful family ruckus, but Jacob is so glad to have his favorite son home again that in time the whole incident blows over and they all live happily ever after.

Such are the wonderful possibilities of science fiction and the time machine. But when we press the control buttons, get "back to the future," and see how it all comes out, we are horrified. Twenty years later when the great famine strikes there is no wise Joseph in Egypt, and no grain to eat. Canaan and Egypt are wiped out by starvation. The Hittites and other savage tribes destroy those whom the famine didn't. A handful of barbarous people set back civilization by centuries. God's plan for His people and the preparation for the Messiah are badly disrupted and delayed. The whole world is different and there are countless worse evils. All because you and I got over-anxious and interfered by killing one mangy Bedouin dog to save an innocent teenager from a lot of trouble.

> *There is nothing so accidental or incidental, so foolish or evil, that God is not able to use it as grist for His providential mill.*

There is no Biblical story which better illustrates the overarching providence of God in our lives than that of Joseph. It tells us that "in all things God works for the good of those who love Him, who have been called according to His purpose" (Romans 8:28). Even in the most unlikely incidents in Joseph's life, God was at work, making them turn out for His purposes. Let me remind you of a few of them:

- Joseph's being sold into slavery took him to Egypt where God had time to make a large nation out of His people, as they lived within Egyptian protection
- Being sold to Potiphar, Captain of the King's Guard, enabled Joseph to become thoroughly Egyptianized and brought him within one step of Pharaoh himself
- Joseph's false arrest and imprisonment, through a spurned wife's unjust accusations, took him to the royal jail where he was to meet Pharaoh's chief servants and interpret their dreams

- Being forgotten by the ungrateful cupbearer for two whole years led to Joseph being remembered at the right moment as the only possible interpreter of Pharaoh's dreams

Thirteen years it had taken. Thirteen terrible and tragic years, filled largely with evil—hate, suffering, darkness, injustice, human failures, and what (to us in our clever time machine) looks like a lot of just plain bad luck. I daresay that if we could, several times we would have jumped into the scene, intervened, and made it come out with a much "happier" ending. Of course, now that we can look back on Joseph's story, we see the great underlying truth—that God is able to work out His purpose even through the sins, crimes, failures, and blunders of human lives. There is nothing so accidental or incidental, so foolish or evil, that God is not able to use it as grist for His providential mill. Yes, hindsight is 20/20. Our optometrists tell us that's the best vision we can have.

50/20 Vision

Joseph had even better vision, though. He combined *sight, foresight,* and *hindsight* into *50/20 vision.* In Genesis 50:20 he tells his brothers, "As for you, you meant evil against me, but God meant it for good" (*RSV*). Joseph's unwavering faith in the God of his dreams caused him to know that God could take the evil which was "intended to harm" him and make it work out not only to help him, but even to help those who meant to harm him. God's redeeming power made their intended evil became the very means God used for "the saving of many lives," including their own!

We Christians need 50/20 vision when it comes to the big picture, that is, the larger events of the world as they make up history. At the darkest moments we need to see that God is always in charge and never loses control of any situation. He is working behind the scenes, carrying out His plans and purposes through people who haven't the slightest notion He is using them in this way. This is evident in the case of the pagan King Cyrus. God said, "He is my shepherd and will accomplish all that I please." He added, "I summon you by name and bestow on you a title of honor, though you do not acknowledge Me" (Isaiah 44:28*a*; 45:4). In the book of Jeremiah, God repeatedly called King Nebuchadnezzar "My servant" (Jeremiah 25:9; 27:6). Cyrus, God's shepherd? Nebuchadnezzar, God's servant? These are ancient names, which may be largely meaningless for us today. Are there any examples from more modern times? Is it possible that God is using the same terms for today's leaders of history? Does He still say, "I am using you, though you do not know Me"?

Most Christians have heard of the great revival which swept Indonesia in the 1960s and 1970s, but few know how it came about. For almost twenty years, from 1945 to 1965, President Sukarno was the champion of independence. He began democratically enough, but gradually he became more and more dictatorial. Although not a Communist himself, he was overfriendly with Red China and Communism. Finally, there were over three million members of the Communist party in his country, making it the third largest in the world. Secretly backed by Beijing, the Communists planned to take over Indonesia in 1967; however, things seemed to be going so successfully they decided to do it ahead of schedule. In October 1965, the Communists launched a coup, captured the President's palace and the radio station, and killed six of the top army generals.

Indonesia is the fifth largest country in the world and stretches in a series of islands 3,000 miles east to west. If the coup had succeeded, Red China and Indonesia would form a massive Communist power block. However, at a critical moment, General Sukarno had gone to spend the night in the hospital with a sick daughter. He escaped death, rallied the army at the last minute, and decisively crushed the revolt.

Then a strange thing happened. The people became outraged and turned against the Communists in savage revenge. In the next two months, there was a mass slaughter of over 400,000 Communist party members. What good could possibly come of this carnage and confusion? Since Indonesia is such a strong Muslim country, you would have thought they would have turned to Islam. But since most of the Communists had previously been Muslims, and since it was now mostly Muslims who were slaughtering the Communists, this was ruled out.

The Christian Indonesians had consistently refused to join in the massacre. They had kept preaching forgiveness and love and the rebuilding of the nation. For this reason, Communists and disillusioned Muslims began to turn to Christianity by the thousands. Muslim military officers, wanting to change the attitude among their own army men, actually distributed thousands of copies of Bible extracts. Another interesting factor is that since Sukarno had forcibly raised literacy from five percent in 1949 to sixty-five percent in 1965 (almost total literacy for people under thirty-five years of age), the military men could all read these Gospel passages and many were converted. The Spirit used all this to revive the existing church, and there took place one of the greatest revival movements in this century—within eighteen months, over a quarter of a million new conversions. By the late 1980s, Indonesia had a church of over ten million, one of the largest in all Asia.

God's providence worked to perform yet another amazing miracle. In 1990, Trans World Radio (TWR), the Christian broadcasting organization, made arrangements to broadcast the Gospel to Europe from a new radio transmitter. They expected to transmit from Moscow, but for many years after World War II, their transmitter had been located in the tiny country of Monaco. This was the land made famous by its rulers, Prince Rainier and Princess Grace, and world-renowned for its gambling resort of Monte Carlo. How did this, the one evangelical voice broadcasting into all Europe and Russia, come to be located in that strange town known primarily for gambling?

Because of its central location, Adolf Hitler had decided to make Monte Carlo the center of his propagandizing of Europe, and he had built a gigantic radio transmitting tower there. After the war was over, the tower was a financial liability, and Monaco offered to lease it to anyone who would pay for it. Paul Freed, president of Trans World Radio, heard about this and felt led of God to make a down payment on it with an option to buy. The balance needed was around $83,000. With only a few days left to pay up, the situation was brought to the attention of Herman Schulte, a wealthy West German industrialist. How did he get into the picture? Mr. Schulte had fought with Hitler's army as a Nazi soldier, and had been wounded and left to die on a battlefield. Some American medics picked him up, and took him to a hospital and saved his life. Then he was shipped to the States and placed in a prisoner-of-war camp in Tennessee. During that time some laypersons from a nearby Baptist church conducted services for the POWs. It was there that Schulte was soundly converted and became a staunch believer. When he heard of the possibility of Paul Freed getting Hitler's giant radio tower in order to broadcast the Gospel, he picked up the bill for the remaining $83,000. Think of it— Hitler had built it for his own evil propaganda purposes, but never used it once. For years it was the only voice reaching all of Europe with the Gospel. But the story isn't over yet.

Some years later, TWR needed a new transmitter. They had been praying for one which would have tremendous power to penetrate anywhere in that part of the world. They finally found one. Sukarno of Indonesia had ordered a radio transmitter to broadcast *his* propaganda throughout all Asia. It had enormous power and was fearfully expensive. After he was thrown out of power, the new government canceled the order. The company stuck with it offered to sell it at less than half price, just to get their investment out of it! Paul Freed and Trans World Radio again prayed the money in and bought it.

Do you get the full picture? The Gospel, beamed to all of Europe with tremendous power, from an enormous transmitter ordered by Sukarno, through a gigantic tower built by Hitler. Let me tell you what I consider the most interesting little detail of the story. (Did I say *little*?) When they moved Sukarno's massive transmitter into the place Hitler had built for one, it was such an exact fit that there was only one inch to spare!

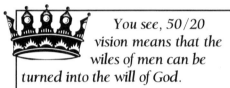

You see, 50/20 vision means that the wiles of men can be turned into the will of God.

Some time ago I heard a Purdue University professor say on TV, "History is essentially the record of unintended consequences." He was only half right. Maybe these consequences are unintended by humans, but by being incorporated into God's purposes, they are intended by the Divine. You see, 50/20 vision means that the wiles of men can be turned into the will of God. When evil seems so triumphant that we tend to become discouraged, we need to remember that God is indeed the Lord of history. Although He is certainly not the Author of everything that happens, He is the *Master* of everything, and will use it to work out His purposes in history.

The great Scottish preacher Alexander Maclaren, commenting on Joseph's life, compares it to the building of a coral reef. The coral polyps knowing nothing of the plan for the reef—that it will someday be a great, beautiful island or simply a lovely ornament to brighten a home—blindly builds the reef from the material supplied by the ocean. In the same way, evildoers and foolish, proud people unknowingly carry out God's purposes. Maclaren says that even sin is made to counteract itself and to become the channel through which the water of life flows. Because of God's sovereignty and His goodness, we find ourselves at the point of success even in enemy territory.

In many instances God's providence brings together seemingly unrelated events and makes them work together for good. In chapter 6, I described the completely unplanned way God had enabled two missionaries to surrender our town to the Indian Army and thus keep many people from being killed. It all happened as Paul Wagner and I walked out of Bidar to see what was happening. As we came up over a small rise, we were suddenly faced with a lone gun carrier, an officer of the advanced unit. He drew his revolver, pointed it straight at us and, with an oath, demanded to know who we were. When I found my voice I said, "We are American missionaries and we're here to help." There was a long pause as he looked us over. Finally he put his gun back in the holster, stuck out his hand and said with a smile, "Oh, Yankees, huh?"

It was not until many hours after the "triumphal entry" into town that we finally had a chance to ask him why he hadn't shot us but suddenly had become so friendly. He explained that during the War he had been stationed 1,500 miles away on the China/Burma/India border, along with soldiers of several nationalities. Because of racial prejudice, some of the foreign officers had looked down on the Indian officers, keeping them segregated and not allowing them into their clubs and athletic events. The Americans, however, had been open and friendly. "Your GI's," he said, "treated us like fellow human beings."

That night as we replayed the day's events, we experienced a lot of fear about what might have happened. We thanked God for those unknown and unknowing GI's, and that God in His providence had linked us all together, as Joseph said, "for the saving of many lives."

In 1989 I held a healing seminar at the military base in Fort Rucker, Alabama. One day we went for the noon meal to the nearby town of Enterprise. They showed me the only monument in the world built in the shape of a bug to honor a bug! Back in 1915, the Mexican boll weevil invaded southeast Alabama and destroyed sixty percent of the cotton crop, the mainstay of the area. In desperation the farmers turned to diversified farming with an emphasis on peanuts. The new crop brought a great wave of unexpected prosperity. By 1917 the county harvested more peanuts than any other county in the nation.

> *Sometimes the tears of history are changed into laughter, after we see the big picture.*

The citizens were so grateful that they erected a monument and on December 11, 1919, dedicated the public marker with this inscription:

> In profound appreciation of the boll weevil,
> And what it has done as the herald of prosperity.

What began as a pestilence ended in praise. What they thought was a great tragedy turned out to be a great blessing. Yes, sometimes the tears of history are changed into laughter, after we see the big picture.

Is God Really "In" Everything?

What about the little picture—the smaller events, the personal and individual details that go into our everyday lives? The story of Joseph confirms the fact that 50/20 vision sees God working even in these. I suppose if Helen and I were to choose the single most important lesson God has taught us through the curriculum of experience, it would be the unshakable conviction that God's participating presence is in every detail of life. We certainly didn't learn that overnight. It took many years of painful lessons for this truth to finally become the bedrock conviction and operating principle of our lives. God, the Divine Optometrist, had to change the prescription of our spiritual lenses several times before we had 50/20 vision for the small print of life.

Paul's oft-quoted words, "Rejoice in the Lord always," remind us that "the Lord is near" (Philippians 4:4-5). Since the older translations read, "The Lord is at hand," for many years we thought this was a reference to the nearness of Christ's second coming. Only gradually did we come to learn it also includes His present-tense presence and really meant, "The Lord is *on* hand." Later in that same chapter Paul says he had "...learned the secret of being content in any and every situation..." (Philippians 4:12). We believe we too have learned the secret, namely, that *God is in everything*. The clearest New Testament statement of 50/20 vision is Romans 8:28. The Phillips translation says it best, "We know that to those who love God, who are called according to his plan, everything that happens fits into a pattern for good."

In her book *Something More*, Catherine Marshall uses this idea as the title of her first chapter, "Yes, God Is in Everything." She frankly admits she borrowed it from Hannah Whitehall Smith's classic, *The Christian's Secret of a Happy Life*. Of course, Hannah borrowed it from a long line of saints and writers, and they obviously got it from Paul's advice to the Philippians to give thanks in everything (Philippians 4:6). She also drew on Paul's words to the Ephesians, "Always giving thanks to God the Father for everything, in the name of our Lord Jesus Christ" (Ephesians 5:20).

In her chapter, Catherine Marshall tells how she resisted Hannah's idea for twenty-seven years after she first read it. She simply could not and would not accept the idea that no matter how frustrating, tragic, evil, or painful the circumstances, no matter what the actual instrumentality was in a particular situation, God was in everything in the sense that He was at work in it to bring about His purposes for good.

Let me be careful to say this does not mean everything that happens in your life is God's ideal will, His perfect and intentional will for you. It isn't. But it *is* to say that nothing can come into your life except by first passing through His permissive will. Just think of this. The very fact it has been filtered through His hands means there is no circumstance, no interruption, no breakage, no loss, no grief, no sin, and no mess so dreadful that God cannot bring "a pattern of good" out of it. It means God is the Divine Alchemist who can take any material—even junk from the rubbish heap of life—and, melting this refuse in the pure fire of His loving purposes, hand it back to us as gold. God is the Divine Strategist who leads us by some unexpected paths into His victory.

Is this also true of the little things—the daily, trivial, seemingly meaningless, and often frustrating circumstances of life? Is the Almighty God really in those events?

Bad Luck and a Wasted Day

Sometimes we speak of "a strange train of circumstances." My "strange train" actually included a train. One day in the early 1950s, during our first term in India, I hurriedly caught the early morning train to attend a committee meeting at another mission station. Since I would be home late that evening, I took very little with me besides some necessary papers and, of course, the ever-present Stanley thermos of boiled drinking water. It was beastly hot, and I didn't want to carry more weight than necessary. However, when we got about halfway to our destination, the train stopped. There had been a derailment up ahead with damage to the tracks. We backed up a few miles and pulled into a small station literally out in the middle of nowhere. There we sat on a siding until the next day when I was finally able to catch the train back to Bidar and home.

I was chagrined to discover that in my haste I had brought nothing to read—not even my constant companion, the Phillips New Testament! I got out and wandered around the railway station. Besides the usual tea and short-order food shop, there was an old and dilapidated Higgenbotham's bookstall—one of the remnants of British India. There didn't seem to be anything in English and, since we had by now traveled into a different language area, even the magazines and books were in a vernacular I didn't know. The shopkeeper, sensing my plight, dug deep into his stock and with a proud smile brought out the lone English book. It was a well-worn paperback edition of *Atlas Shrugged* by Ayn Rand. Although at the time I had never even heard of either the book or the author, it seemed my only hope. I must admit its unique style, and its incredible anti-Christian philosophy of selfishness through its 1,100 pages kept me occupied for that hot and otherwise boring day. As far as I was concerned, though, it was all just plain lousy luck and a wasted day and a half. (As a result, when I got back home I grumped around and made life more difficult for Helen.)

Ten years later, in my first year as pastor of the host church to the Asbury institutions, a young student phoned to make an appointment with me. He said he was a sophomore at Asbury College and "was having some serious intellectual problems regarding the Christian faith." As soon as he sat down in my office, I sensed his discomfort. Obviously a brilliant pre-med student, he looked down his sophomoric nose at me with an expression of combined disdain and pity. I could almost read his thoughts: "I can see I've come to the wrong person to get help with this kind of problem. He seems like a nice enough guy and may have been all right as a missionary, but the poor man certainly wouldn't understand the kind of stuff *I* need to talk about."

He kept the conversation on a surface level until his attitude began to get to me. In my insecurity I could feel myself slumping lower and lower in my chair. Finally I asked him about the intellectual questions he had mentioned over the phone. He was still reluctant, but he finally told me it involved some books he had read which had "shook him up." I suggested that we could discuss the books and his doubts. At this he was even more hesitant, beat around the bush for awhile, but at last said with a kind of hopeless sigh, "Well, I don't suppose you've ever heard of a book called *Atlas Shrugged* by Ayn Rand?"

I straightened up in the chair, smiled, and rising to the full height of my erudition replied, "Of course, I've heard of it. In fact I read it years ago, all 1,100 pages of it. She's quite a writer, isn't she?" The student was completely shocked; his lower jaw dropped and his defenses followed suit. We had a long discussion about Ayn Rand and other similar authors whose aggressively anti-Christian philosophies were popular during the 1960s. Best of all, it was the beginning of a close friendship and a mentoring relationship for the next two years which helped establish him in a solid Christian faith—a faith still evident in his many years as a practicing physician. And it all began with a seemingly accidental circumstance, a very frustrating interruption—something I had considered bad luck and a wasted day. It took me ten years to learn how wrong I had been and how God had truly been *in* the situation.

In the Bigger Ones Too

There are those bigger but equally personal situations which involve major decisions, circumstances which force changes of careers and continents, and even the callings of God Himself—changes which are wrenching, crunching, disorienting, painful. If we think that the little ones are too trivial and simple for God, maybe the bigger ones are too twisted and complex for Him.

It was Christmastime and we were in the parsonage at Bangalore where I was the missionary pastor of the English-speaking church. Our kids were home from Kodai—the American boarding school in the hills of South India, which they attended from January to November. Helen was at the piano, and we were gathered around singing together—one of our favorite family pastimes. I happened to look over at our twelve-year-old son, Steve. His sloppy posture bugged me. "Stand up straight," I ordered.

"I am standing up straight, Dad."

"No you're not." I was getting put out with him.

"Honest, Dad, I am," he protested. I kept looking at his belt. It slanted down a full two inches on his left side.

"Wait a minute, Steve. Just stand there like that." I went over to the piano, got our Methodist Hymnal and put it under his left foot. Although the book was more than an inch thick, his belt still sloped downward. I added another songbook until his belt was in a straight line. It had taken two full inches to level up both legs. The music stopped, Helen looked over at Steve, and then she and I stared at each other. It dawned on both of us about the same time. In a recent spurt of growth, his right leg had outgrown his left leg by two inches. Three years prior to this, when we had left the States, the orthopedist had warned us of this possible complication from a problem which had begun at birth.

We took him to an American specialist in India, who told us that Steve required complicated surgery and at least three years of close observation. This care would not be available within India. That would mean our ministry in India was over, for in those days if missionaries stayed out past the one-year validity of their "no objection to return" permit, they could not get back into the country. In a matter of a few weeks we saw our calling and commitment to a lifetime career as missionaries brought to an end.

What should we do? Our daughter Sharon was in her senior year of high school and would graduate in May. We decided that I would stay in India, keeping our daughters Sharon and Debbie in Kodai, while Helen would fly home with Steve for his operation. I would continue the work until

Sharon's graduation, then pack up and come home for good. I would ask the bishop in Kentucky for an appointment and start all over again as a pastor in the United States.

This was the background of our tearful farewell at the Bombay airport. As we kissed good-bye and wept in one another's arms, Helen said to me, "David, the thing that worries me most is wondering if you can ever be happy except as a missionary in India."

I replied, "Honey, you're right. This is my call from God. I can never be happy doing anything else." At the time we thought our words were very profound and deeply spiritual. We were being faithful to our call. I felt God must surely be impressed.

However, when we look back at that pious and tearful farewell in the Bombay airport, we have to laugh at ourselves. We realize those words were pure and unadulterated spiritual baloney. We were very sincere and very ignorant. Weren't our words faithful to a call? No! They were an expression of our depression, spoken out of unconscious unbelief and selfish spiritual stupidity. Most of all, our tears were clouding our 50/20 vision. We only saw our missionary dreams being destroyed. We were failing to see God in everything, working out His pattern for good. We had no idea that God was going to open a whole new ministry for us. We never imagined it would turn out to be the beginning of one of the happiest and most reward-ing times of our lives. We never dreamed it would be the beginning of a new and brighter dream, resulting in a worldwide ministry through writing.

The promise in Psalm 59:9*b*-10*a* has always meant a lot to us. "You, O God, are my fortress, my loving God. God will go before me." But the full import of its meaning came when we read Leslie Weatherhead's transla-tion, "My God, in His lovingkindness, shall meet me at every corner." Corners represent turning points, places of uncertainty and change around which an unknown future awaits us. We have learned that God is not only in everything but also around every corner. Years ago I found this little saying and have kept it before me:

> He is already around the corner to meet me,
> So I can enter the future unafraid
> For nothing can come to me
> that cannot be used
> by the *grace* of God,
> for the *glory* of God,
> my own *growth*,
> and the *good* of others.

The Eyes of the Heart

In Ephesians 1:18-19, Paul seems to mix his metaphors when he prays "that the eyes of your heart may be enlightened in order that you may know the hope to which He has called you, the riches of His glorious inheritance in the saints, and His incomparably great power for us who believe." Actually, Paul is simply recognizing that the 50/20 vision we have been describing does not depend on the refractions of our eyes, but on the reflections of our hearts. Our physical eyes decide what we see, but it is our inner eyes, the eyes of our heart, which determine what we perceive in what we see. How we interpret the sight depends on the spirit in which we look at it.

We learn from Joseph that to live out our dreams requires 50/20 vision, and for that we need certain qualities of spirit:

A realistic spirit. Young Joseph was certainly a dreamer, but when those dreams ran right into the realities of a cruel and unjust world, he never wasted energy by escaping into an unreal world of fantasy. He always took the actual materials provided for him in his particular situation and used them to help build his dream.

> *50/20 vision does not depend on the refractions of our eyes, but on the reflections of our hearts.*

George Washington Carver used to tell this story about himself. One day while walking out in a field he said to God, "Mr. Creator, why did You make this universe?"

God replied, "Little man, that question's much too big for you."

"Well then, Mr. Creator, why did You make the human race?"

Again came the answer, "Little man, even that one's way too big for you."

Carver's eye fell on a peanut plant. "All right then, tell me why did You make the peanut?"

This time God said, "Little man, that's just about your size. Listen, and I'll tell you." Carver did just that; he developed over 300 different ways to use the peanut and helped to revolutionize the economy of the South.

With 50/20 vision, we can be visionary but not unrealistic. It perceives way beyond what it sees, but it never denies what it does see. It takes a hard, realistic look at facts: failures, sins, handicaps, broken dreams, damaged emotions, accidents, tragedies, pain, suffering, and death. God wants to help many of us find fulfillment in revised, reshaped, and reconstructed dreams; but He cannot do it because we keep clinging to unrealistic and unrealizable dreams by mourning their loss. Joseph never once said, "If only ...." He always asked, "How can I best serve my God in this place?" With 50/20 vision, we need never waste emotional energy and spiritual strength in attempting to build dreams out of fantasy materials like options which no longer exist.

I can hear someone objecting, "But surely God does not need our sins, our mistakes, and our blunders, or those that other people committed against us, in order to work out His plans and purposes." Of course, He doesn't. But in this fallen and imperfect world, those are just about all the materials He has to work with. Many of us have not had the opportunity of choosing the materials. Our only choice is in what we will *do* with them.

On February 23, 1986, Mrs. Jane MacCall was interviewed on NBC television. Her husband was a Christian psychiatrist who had been murdered—shot four times in the head by a mentally deranged patient whom he had been treating. The interviewer asked how she could possibly have coped with such a senseless tragedy. She answered, "I decided life is a multiple-choice exam. I was faced with the choices, 'Fold up and go under,' or 'Face it and go forward.' I decided by God's help to face it and keep going forward."

A forgiving spirit. The eyes of a resentful and revengeful heart are never able to see God at work in all things. One of our common, everyday expressions recognizes this: "I was so mad I couldn't see straight." Yes, bitterness blurs vision. Some of us need to be freed from smoldering resentments over our own personal tragedies and handicaps.

In 1989, Billy Graham preached in the giant sports stadium in Budapest, Hungary to 110,000 people, the largest crowd in the stadium's history. The person whose witness was the most effective to those people—who for so many years had suffered oppression and imprisonment—was Joni Earickson Tada. She sang and shared with great power what the cross meant to her. They understood when, free from all bitterness and self-pity, she pointed to her wheelchair and said, "This is the prison which has set me free."

50/20 vision requires lenses wiped clean from all smudges of bitterness and hate.

A forgiving spirit reaches toward those who have wronged and hurt us. Ted Morris was the only child of Frank and Elizabeth Morris. In December 1982, Ted, an eighteen-year-old college student from southwestern Kentucky, was killed by a twenty-four-year-old drunken driver named Tommy Pigage. Tommy was arrested and charged with murder, since his blood-alcohol content was three times higher than the legal level. The first time the Morrises saw him, they hated him. Here he was, walking and talking and breathing, and their son was in a fresh grave because of him. They felt he had no right to live. They were happy when he began serving a five-year prison term, but slowly a spirit of forgiveness began to work in their hearts. They requested permission for Tommy to be released from jail into their custody every Sunday so they could get to know him. Finally, they were able to completely forgive him. A picture in *Parade*, November 16, 1986, shows the Morrises with their arms around Tommy. "He's our friend now. We can't say he's like a son because no one could ever take Ted's place. But we love Tommy ... like a nephew." What brought about the change in spirit? They didn't want their son's death to be in vain. It was only as they found grace to forgive that they were able to see meaning and purpose working through the terrible loss. Using 50/20 vision requires lenses wiped clean from all smudges of bitterness and hate.

A trusting spirit. It is no surprise that Joseph is mentioned in the great Faith Hall of Fame in Hebrews 11. His 50/20 vision included the daring faith to see plan and purpose in all those seemingly irrational events. Trust dares to believe that God can take the worst materials and turn them into good. It dares to project meaning into meaninglessness, purpose into the seemingly accidental. No, it doesn't gloss over evil like a cloudy-minded Hinduism or a soft-headed New Age-ism. It looks evil straight in the face and recognizes it to be evil, but then declares that God can turn it for good. In fact, the faith of 50/20 vision dares to say that the only lasting evil in the world is that of our inner resentful and unbelieving attitudes. It tells us that good and evil are not in our circumstances but in the way we react to them. The bottom line of this trust is that nothing is so evil that it can ever go beyond God's ability to refashion, reshape, recycle, and redirect it for His purposes. He has planned success for us, regardless of any circumstances that might intervene, any obstacles that are thrown in our way, any battles we must fight.

Although many years have passed, I still remember the day when Lucille, a woman in her early thirties, shared her story with me. Before she spoke, her nervousness and tense frown revealed her pain. Recent stressful events had dredged up a collage of multicolored memories—

greens of jealousy, yellows of fear, reds of abuse and anger, blues of depression, and grays of doubt and confusion. She described an extremely dysfunctional family with an alcoholic father. She had not been physically abused personally, but she had regularly witnessed his abuse of her mother.

Lucille had had no religious influences in her growing years. The family did not go to church and, to this day, continues to oppose Lucille's Christian life. That's what made her story so unusual. She kept saying, "I can't understand it, let alone explain it, but from around five years of age I just always knew God was with me." She went on to relate that during high school she had finally surrendered to the God who had been seeking her for so long. Then she had gotten away from Him for a period in her life. Unfortunately, during that time she had done what many children of alcoholics unconsciously do—married an alcoholic. He was so abusive that in a matter of months she had to get out of the marriage, but the trauma of the disillusionment and ensuing divorce had led her back to the Lord and a deeper relationship with Him. So where was the devastating ambush by doubts about God and her own self-worth coming from?

She had never made genuine peace with her whole family background; and there was one especially unforgettable incident. When Lucille was eleven years old and the youngest of five children, her mother called a family conference to announce that she was once again pregnant. Lucille's father suggested that the mother could have an abortion—and then came the bombshell. Her mother said abortion was out of the question. She and her husband had actually agreed on one when she was expecting Lucille. Since abortion was not legal at that time, they had somehow scraped up the money for her to fly to a Caribbean country to have it done. But at the very last minute, while prepped and lying on the operating table, she changed her mind and told the doctors she could not go through with it. She had to argue the angry medical team out of proceeding with the abortion.

As the eleven-year-old Lucille listened to this, she almost went into shock. But no one was allowed to discuss the matter.

That memorable scene haunted her for years, overwhelming her with the thought that she had not been wanted. She pushed it out of her mind and never came to terms with it. I asked her to put on her 50/20 lenses and take a new look at the whole incident. We went back to that

Caribbean hospital table and asked the ultimate question, "Where was God? You keep saying He's been with you since you were five. Don't we need to revise this to say that you have been on His schedule since long before then? In fact, according to His Word, you were there before the creation of the world itself" (Ephesians 1:4). As we shared and prayed, the story of John Wesley seemed to help. When Wesley was a boy of six, he was rescued from his burning house just seconds before the roof crashed in. All of his life he spoke of himself as "a brand plucked from the burning," and wanted this phrase carved on his tombstone.

Lucille was finally able to forgive and relinquish the hurt, humiliation, and anger over her family life—the results of other people's sinful choices. In this way she came to see her whole life through the cleansed, clear lenses of 50/20 vision. In our final time together, her bitterness and doubts had turned to thanksgiving, and she was filled with "wonder, love, and praise." Lucille, an unusually bright, beautiful, and gifted "life plucked from the abortionist's table," is now the wife of a pastor.

We have called Genesis 50:20 the Romans 8:28 of the Old Testament. Let me suggest that you read Romans 8:28-34. With a marking pen, underline the eleven great verbs in the passage. They are verbs of God's action toward us: works (Romans 8:28); foreknew and predestined (Romans 8:29); called, justified, and glorified (Romans 8:30); did not spare but gave (Romans 8:32); died, was raised to life, and is interceding (Romans 8:34).

Now read Romans 8:35-39, underlining the seventeen nouns in the passage. They are the most terrifying nouns that evil can throw against us: trouble, hardship, persecution, famine, nakedness, danger, or sword (Romans 8:35); death, life, angels, demons, the present, the future, powers (Romans 8:38); height, depth, or anything else in all creation (Romans 8:39).

Notice, the seventeen deadly nouns cannot take us beyond the power of the eleven divine verbs. In fact, the seventeenth noun is all-inclusive, "anything else in all creation." Thus, there is absolutely nothing that is "able to separate us from the love of God that is in Christ Jesus our Lord" (Romans 8:39).

This is a powerful passage upon which to meditate. The dream-destroyers, the dream-stealers, and those who break, seduce, and attempt to imprison us ultimately cannot keep us from succeeding—even though we seem to be trapped, for a time, in enemy territory. The God who created the world and filled us with His precious dreams holds us close in His loving and powerful arms.

> Thy calmness bends serene above,
> My restlessness to still;
> Around me flows Thy quickening life,
> To nerve my faltering will;
> Thy presence fills my solitude;
> Thy providence turns all to good.
>
> Embosomed deep in Thy dear love,
> Held in Thy law I stand;
> Thy hand in all things I behold
> And all things in Thy hand;
> Thou leadest me by unsought ways,
> And turn'st my mourning into praise.[1]
> —Samuel Longfellow

NOTES

Chapter One

1. Bob Richards, *The Heart of a Champion* (Westwood, New Jersey: Fleming Revell, 1959), 21-24.

Chapter Three

1. Donald Wildmon and Randall Nulton, *Don Wildmon, The Man the Networks Love To Hate* (Wilmore, Kentucky: Bristol Books, 1989).

2. Oswald Chambers, *God's Workmanship* (Fort Washington, Pennsylvania: Christian Literature Crusade, 1953), 59.

3. Oswald Chambers, *Christian Discipline*, Vol. 2 (Fort Washington, Pennsylvania: Christian Literature Crusade, 1936), 55.

Chapter Six

1. A. W. Tozer, *The Root of the Righteous* (Chicago: Moody Press, 1955), 127.

2. James Weldon Johnson, *The Creation*.

Chapter Seven

1. F. B. Meyer, *Joseph* (Fort Washington, Pennsylvania: Christian Literature Crusade, n.d.), 62.

Chapter Eight

1. E. Stanley Jones, *Christ and Human Suffering* (London: Hodder and Stoughton, 1933), 180-181.

2. Rosamond E. Herklots, "Forgive Our Sins As We Forgive," *The United Methodist Hymnal*, 1989, 390.

Chapter Nine

1. David Seamands, *Putting Away Childish Things* (Wheaton, Illinois: Victor Books, 1982), 143.

Chapter Ten

1. Samuel Longfellow, "I Look to Thee in Every Need" *The United Methodist Book of Hymns*, 1964, 219.

Fulfill the desires of your heart

God planted dreams in you for a reason – your dreams really can come true!

There is no better Biblical story for understanding the process of seeing your dreams fulfilled than the life of Joseph. Doug Murren takes you to the heart of seeing your dreams fulfilled.

This inspiring book will renew and refresh you to pursue your dreams. With *Achieving Your Dreams – The Joseph Factor*, your dreams really can come true.

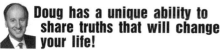

Doug has a unique ability to share truths that will change your life!

"Doug is one of today's finest young pastors/leaders and writers. He is uniquely gifted with an ability to capture the timelessness of truth and press it to the soul of today's circumstances to answer hurt or to beget hope–or both!" – Jack Hayford, Senior Pastor, The Church on the Way

A great book for all of us who dream big dreams

"The world scoffs at dreamers. God doesn't. He speaks to them. Doug Murren has written a practical, relevant book for all of us who want to dream big dreams for God and see them through."
– Michele Buckingham, former Managing Editor, Ministries Today Magazine

Achieving Your Dreams by Doug Murren

ISBN: 1-883906-35-0 **Only $9.97**

Code #PUBS110

Change Your Money Stream –

Learn why money flows to some people and away from others

"This is the best financial teaching I've ever heard. I've used these principles for years. Finally, someone who teaches them from the Bible."
- Johnny Berguson, President of Kingdom, Inc. (Listed by *Inc. Magazine* as one of America's 500 fastest growing companies)

This is arguably the best financial book ever written. Mallonee goes to the root of finances. He explains from the Bible why money flows to some people and away from others.

Whether you have $5, $50, or $100,000, the Biblical principles in *Foolproof Finances* will work for you. These proven principles will help you get out of debt, or flourish when you're already doing well. This book will help anyone significantly improve their finances. Discover how you can be financially free.

Hardcover

Foolproof Finances by David Mallonee

ISBN: 1-883906-11-3 **Only $14.97**

Code #PUBS110

Available at your local Christian bookstore or call toll free (800) 597-1123

How to thrive even in chaos!

Discover how you can avoid "paradigm shock"

Change is a part of life. However, shifting paradigms can make you feel overwhelmed and out of control. Whether you're a pastor, church leader, small group leader, Sunday school teacher, or other lay leader you need to be able to manage change successfully.

Learn to anticipate change, cushion transitions, and redirect focus. Find out why even crisis-initiated changes do not have to be negative.

The experts listen to his leadership principles

"I read everything that Doug writes. Why? Because he is a pastor with an effective hand on today and a leader's eye on tomorrow. What he writes about works."

– John Maxwell, Author of bestselling books including *Developing the Leader Within You*

"...Pastor Doug Murren gives you answers you can begin to implement immediately."

– C. Peter Wagner, Author and Professor of Church Growth, Fuller Theological Seminary

Leadershift by Doug Murren

ISBN: 1-883906-30-X **Only $9.97**

Code #PUBS110

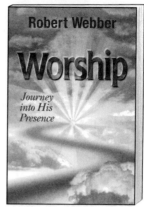

Worship can be the most exciting thing in your life!

Join Robert Webber on the journey in this book. Your worship will never be the same.

You'll discover hidden treasure in this fascinating look at Scripture. You'll find yourself and your church in the journey Dr. Webber paints for you.

No one can help you understand true worship in its rich historical context better than Robert Webber. He takes you on a journey into the very presence of God.

This book will help you experience the presence of God

"I highly recommend Worship: Journey into His Presence; *this book will help you connect with the presence of God and increase your interaction with Jesus.* – LaMar Boschman, Author and Dean of The Worship Institute

Experience the fullness of worship

"Robert Webber helps us realize that worship is more than an inviting concept or an effective technique. It is a journey towards God's presence, into God's presence, and then–through God's presence–toward effective ministry in the world. – Jack Taylor, President of Dimensions Ministries, and author of *Hallelujah Factor*

Worship: Journey Into His Presence by Robert Webber

ISBN: 1-883906-31-8 **Only $9.97**

Code #PUBS110

Available at your local Christian bookstore or call toll free (800) 597-1123

Get the only Bible on Cassette that you can copy and give away

Suddenly you can give copies of the New Testament on Cassette to friends. Make a copy for your school. Copy several for your outreach ministry.

Or copy it for any ministry reason you want and give it away – you won't pay one cent in royalty fees! (We just ask that you don't copy the tapes for resale or profit.) Never before has anyone, anywhere made the Bible on cassette so easily available to so many.

Two years of planning was put into this Bible on Cassette before any production started.

Unique features of The Classic℠ King James Version

- The only Bible on Cassette you can copy and give away!
- 16 Free Access℠ studio quality master cassettes of the New Testament
- Recorded at the perfect speed for comprehension and enjoyment (It's not jam-packed onto 12 cassettes to save money)
- Digitally recorded to prevent listener fatigue
- Features the phenomenal voice of Dr. Vernon Lapps

16 Master Cassettes of the New Testament

The Classic℠ King James Version Bible on Cassette
narrated by Dr. Vernon Lapps

ISBN: 1-883906-14-8 **Only $47.00**

Code #PUBS110

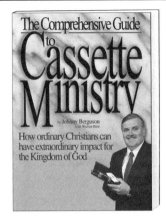

Discover how ordinary Christians can multiply the effectiveness of their whole church!

"This book was so good I could hardly put it down. This book showed me how to do everything... plus it's an abundant source of ideas. I thank God for putting this book in my hands. And I truly believe cassette ministry is a God given tool..."
– Carol Faust, Florida

As you catch the vision for cassette ministry, you'll quickly discover how to help make your entire church more effective through cassette ministry.

That's right. Anyone, anywhere can help make their ENTIRE church more effective through cassette ministry. You won't find another book like this anywhere!

The Comprehensive Guide to Cassette Ministry is loaded with practical ideas that will help you increase the effectiveness of nearly every ministry in your church. You'll discover four compelling Biblical reasons to do cassette ministry, the right – and wrong – ways to do it; how to fund your tape ministry; how to increase evangelism, teaching, and pastoral care through cassettes. You'll learn everything you could possibly want to know.

This book is helping ordinary Christians everywhere help make their entire church more effective!

The Comprehensive Guide to Cassette Ministry by Johnny Berguson

ISBN: 1-883906-12 **Only $19.97**

Code #PUBS110

Available at your local Christian bookstore or call toll free (800) 597-1123

Discover the keys to effective prayer and intercession!

Intercessors, prayer warriors, and praying Christians everywhere are discovering prayer in a fresh, powerful way. *Prayer Audio Magazine™* will catapult your prayer and intercession to new levels.

Pray with greater fervency and power! Get the best of *Prayer Audio Magazine* today!

"Prayer Audio Magazine *challenges us to keep pressing in to God. It keeps us informed, and brings us together to bond in prayer…*" – Pastor Jim Ottman, Maine

The best of *Prayer Audio Magazine:*

- 12 audio cassettes featuring the world's leading authorities on prayer and intercession – these are 12 of the best issues ever of *Prayer Audio Magazine*
- 12 helpful listening guides (one for each cassette)
- Deluxe storage binder stores all 12 cassettes and listening guides
- Exclusive interviews and more
- Noted speakers include: Judson Cornwall, C. Peter Wagner, and Eddie & Alice Smith

Only ~~$97~~ $87 with coupon or
special code on coupon + $9.97 shipping
60-Day Money Back Guarantee

Call toll free (800) 597-1123

Experience new depths in worship!

Invite the world's leading authorities into your own home through *Worship Audio Magazine™*. Each cassette contains key messages, exclusive interviews, and more.

With the best of *Worship Audio Magazine*, you'll find yourself moving to new depths of insight and worship experience!

"*…up-to-date spiritual manna…I am very pleased…*" – Mike Kelly, Tennessee

"Worship Audio Magazine *has expanded my understanding… The messages are greatly complemented by the personal interviews.*" – Karen Hiller, New York

The best of *Worship Audio Magazine:*

- 12 of the best audio cassette issues ever of *Worship Audio Magazine* – hear from some of the most anointed men and women of our generation
- 12 listening guides (one for each tape)
- Deluxe storage binder stores all cassettes and listening guides
- Exclusive interviews and more
- Noted speakers include: Robert Webber, Judson Cornwall, LaMar Boschman, and Bob Mumford

Only ~~$97~~ $87 with coupon or
special code on coupon + $9.97 shipping
60-Day Money Back Guarantee

Call toll free (800) 597-1123